GOD
IN NEW TESTAMENT
THEOLOGY

The Library of Biblical Theology

Leo Perdue
General Editor and Old Testament Editor

James D. G. Dunn
New Testament Editor

Michael Welker
Systematic Theology Editor

LIBRARY OF BIBLICAL THEOLOGY

GOD

IN NEW TESTAMENT THEOLOGY

LARRY W. HURTADO

Abingdon Press
Nashville

GOD IN NEW TESTAMENT THEOLOGY

Copyright © 2010 by Abingdon Press

This book is printed on acid-free paper.

Library of Congress Cataloging-in-Publication Data

Hurtado, Larry W., 1943-
God in New Testament theology / Leo Perdue, general editor and Old Testament editor ; James D.G. Dunn, New Testament editor ; Michael Welker, systematic theology editor ; God in New Testament theology, Larry W. Hurtado.
p. cm. — (Library of Biblical theology)
Includes bibliographical references.
ISBN 978-0-687-46545-3 (book-pbk./trade pbk., binding, adhesive : alk. paper)
1. God—Biblical teaching. 2. Bible. N.T.—Theology. I. Perdue, Leo G. II. Dunn, James D. G., 1939–
III. Welker, Michael, 1947– IV. Title.
BS2398.H87 2010
231—dc22   2010032899

All other Scripture quotations are the author's translation.

10 11 12 13 14 15 16 17 18 19—10 9 8 7 6 5 4 3 2 1

MANUFACTURED IN THE UNITED STATES OF AMERICA

*To colleagues in New College,
University of Edinburgh,
past and present*

CONTENTS

ABBREVIATIONS

1 En.	*1 Enoch*
1QH	*Hôdayôt* or The Hymns Scroll
1QS	*Serek Hayaḥad* or *Rule of the Community*
AB	Anchor Bible
ABD	*Anchor Bible Dictionary.* Edited by D. N. Freedman. 6 vols. New York, 1992
AGJU	Arbeiten zur Geschichte des antiken Judentums und des Urchristentums
AJEC	Ancient Judaism and Early Christianity
ANF	*Ante-Nicene Fathers*
Autol.	*Ad Autolycum*
BR	*Biblical Research*
BTB	*Biblical Theology Bulletin*
BTZ	*Berliner Theologische Zeitschrift*
BZNW	Beihefte zur Zeitschrift für die neutestamentliche Wissenschaft
DJG	*Dictionary of Jesus and the Gospels.* Edited by J. B. Green and S. McKnight. Downers Grove, 1992
DLNT	*Dictionary of the Later New Testament and Its Developments.* Edited by R. P. Martin and P. H. Davids. Downers Grove, 1997
DPL	*Dictionary of Paul and His Letters.* Edited by G. F. Hawthorne and R. P. Martin. Downers Grove, 1993
EDNT	*Exegetical Dictionary of the New Testament.* Edited by H. Balz and G. Schneider. English Translation. Grand Rapids, 1990–1993
EEC	*Encyclopedia of Early Christianity.* Edited by E. Ferguson. 2d ed. New York, 1990
ExpTim	*Expository Times*

FRLANT	Forschungen zur Religion und Literatur des Alten und Neuen Testaments
Gig.	*De gigantibus*
HBT	*Horizons in Biblical Theology*
HTS	Harvard Theological Studies
ICC	International Critical Commentary
JBL	*Journal of Biblical Literature*
JHS	*Journal of Hellenic Studies*
JPSSup	Journal of Pentecostal Studies Supplements
JSJSup	Supplements to the Journal for the Study of Judaism
JSNT	*Journal for the Study of the New Testament*
JSNTSup	Journal for the Study of the New Testament: Supplement Series
JTS	*Journal of Theological Studies*
Jub.	*Jubilees*
LXX	Septuagint
Mart. Pol.	*Martyrdom of Polycarp*
MT	Masoretic Text, Hebrew Bible
NICNT	New International Commentary on the New Testament
NIDNTT	*New International Dictionary of New Testament Theology.* Edited by C. Brown. 4 vols. Grand Rapids, 1975–1985
NIDOTTE	*New International Dictionary of Old Testament Theology and Exegesis.* Edited by W. A VanGemeren. 5 vols. Grand Rapids, 1997.
NIGTC	New International Greek Testament Commentary
NovT	*Novum Testamentum*
NovTSup	Supplements to Novum Testamentum
NT	New Testament
NTS	*New Testament Studies*
OT	Old Testament
Prax.	*Adversus Praxean*
PTR	*Princeton Theological Review*
RBL	*Review of Biblical Literature*
SBLDS	Society of Biblical Literature Dissertation Series
SP	Sacra pagina
StBL	Studies in Biblical Literature
SUNT	Studien zur Umwelt des Neuen Testaments

TDNT	*Theological Dictionary of the New Testament.* Edited by G. Kittel and G. Friedrich. Translated by G. W. Bromiley. 10 vols. Grand Rapids, 1964–1976
TGl	*Theologie und Glaube*
ThWAT	*Theologisches Wörterbuch zum Alten Testament.* Edited by G. J. Botterweck and H. Ringgren. Stuttgart, 1970–
TLOT	*Theological Lexicon of the Old Testament.* Edited by E. Jenni, with assistance from C. Westermann. Translated by M. E. Biddle. 3 vols. Peabody, Mass., 1997
TU	Texte und Untersuchungen
WBC	Word Biblical Commentaries
WMANT	Wissenschaftliche Monographien zum Alten und Neuen Testament
WUNT	Wissenschaftliche Untersuchungen zum Neuen Testament

PREFACE

T his modest-sized volume was written during my three-year term as Head of the School of Divinity, University of Edinburgh, and so had to be fitted into available time amid the many administrative responsibilities of that office. Consequently, the original deadline for this book had to be extended, and I am grateful to the editors of this series and Abingdon Press for their patience. Having devoted a number of publications over the last couple of decades to early devotion to Jesus, the invitation from my friend Jimmy Dunn to write this book on "God" presented me an intriguing opportunity to probe more widely into the religious discourse in the fascinating texts that make up the New Testament. I hope that the results of my own investigation and reflections presented here will be stimulating to others, whether fellow scholars, formal students, or the wider public.

I was able to try out earlier drafts of some of the chapters to various audiences. Among these opportunities, I mention in particular the 2008 Kermit Zarley Lectures (North Park University, Chicago) and the 2009 Chen Su Lan Lectures (Trinity Theological College, Singapore), and I record my gratitude to colleagues in both settings who made my visits comfortable and stimulating.

As I write this preface, I also reflect on fourteen years in New College (School of Divinity). For me, this has been a wonderful time of participation in one of the strongest academic centers in the study of theology and religion in the world. In addition to the many attractions of the city of Edinburgh, the scholarly resources in the university and my colleagues in New College have combined to make these very pleasant and productive years. I am pleased to dedicate this book to my New College colleagues (past and present, some of whom, sadly, are deceased, among whom my frequent lunch partner, Andy Ross, I particularly miss), who befriended my wife and me and have continued to make New College such an enjoyable venue for scholarly work.

New College, August 2010

INTRODUCTION

A CURIOUS NEGLECT

I n an essay originally published in 1975, Nils Dahl drew attention to the curious neglect of "God" in New Testament studies. I cite his own words:

> For more than a generation, the majority of New Testament scholars have not only eliminated direct references to God from their works but have also neglected detailed and comprehensive investigation of statements about God. Whereas a number of major works and monographs deal with the Christology (or ecclesiology, eschatology, etc.) of the New Testament, it is hard to find any comprehensive or penetrating study of the theme "God in the New Testament."[1]

Early in the 1990s I had my own discovery of the paucity of studies on "God" in the NT when I agreed to write an article on "God" in the Gospels for a dictionary.[2] Searching then through the previous twenty years of *New Testament Abstracts*, I was able to find only a small handful of publications (and these only journal articles) that directly treated "God" in any of the four canonical Gospels. This meant an unusually short bibliography for a large article (something for which, in a sense, one could be grateful!), but it also reflected the sort of neglect that Dahl decried.

In the following chapter, I consider the state of the matter in the years since Dahl's landmark essay. It is appropriate to ask again at this point how "God" figures in NT scholarship, especially in the last few decades. As we will see, there have been important contributions on this topic. Moreover, there are significant issues that are raised in considering how to address the topic. Before we directly engage these matters, however, we should explore a bit further what prompted Dahl's complaint.

Considering factors in modern NT scholarship that helped account for the neglect of "God," Dahl alleged a "pronounced Christocentricity" among scholars, with roots in the nineteenth century, along with a linked "reaction against metaphysical theology" that goes back even as far as Luther and that was reinforced in the twentieth century by developments such as "demythologizing" and "existential interpretation."[3] That is, the entirely understandable theological emphasis, from the Reformation onward, that we can know God properly not from general philosophical premises but only through reflecting on God's actions toward us (*Deus pro nobis*) has meant that studies of New Testament theology concentrated above all on Jesus (Christology) as the principal agent of divine purposes and on divine redemptive provision (soteriology), the formation of an elect people (ecclesiology), and the ultimate triumph of God's redemptive intentions (eschatology). So, whether deliberately or inadvertently, the topic of "God" was typically subsumed under these other topics and was not often a focus in itself.

Dahl also cited several major scholars of the time, of various critical and theological standpoints (Bultmann, Cullmann, and G. E. Ladd), as illustrative of the view that there was really little to say about "God" as a topic of its own in the NT. In this sort of view, the alleged neglect of "God" is simply an appropriate reflection of the limited place of "God" as a subject in the NT writings. Some of Cullmann's introductory comments in his classic study of NT Christology will serve as an example of this widespread scholarly view. Rightly emphasizing that the oldest confessional expressions preserved in the NT focus on *Jesus'* significance (e.g., "Jesus is Lord," Rom 10:9-10; 1 Cor 12:3; Phil 2:11), Cullmann contended that this meant that "the theological thinking of the first Christians proceeds from Christ, not from God." A few paragraphs later, Cullmann wrote, "We can therefore say that early Christian theology is in reality almost exclusively Christology."[4]

As Dahl observed, however, Cullmann seems not to have noticed that "this statement might also be formulated the other way around."[5] That is, the NT christological affirmations are typically also statements about God's actions and purposes, whether it is sending Jesus (e.g., Gal 4:4-5) or designating his death as redemptive (e.g., Rom 3:25-26; 8:32) or raising Jesus from death and exalting him to heavenly glory (e.g., Acts 2:36; 4:10; Phil 2:9-11) or designating Jesus as the one to whom all things are to be subjected (e.g., 1 Cor 15:27-28; Heb 2:5-13). Moreover, Jesus' own high status and significance are typically expressed with reference to God, as, for example, in lauding Jesus as God's "Son" (e.g., Rom 1:3-4; 1 Thess 1:9-10), the "image" of God who reflects God's own glory (2 Cor 3:18; 4:4-6; Heb 1:3), and the divine Word who comprises the definitive revelation of God (John 1:1-18). In short, just about every christological statement is at the same time a profoundly *theological* statement as well.

To be sure, the key impetus for the development of religious devotion and thought that we see in the NT arises from the impact of Jesus and events and experiences that ensued in the earliest period after his execution, which generated the key conviction that "God" had raised Jesus from death and exalted him to heavenly glory. Unquestionably, christological convictions were central in earliest Christian faith. But the specific content of NT christological thought and the specific shape of the devotional practice reflected in the NT as well also involve quite specific convictions and claims about this God.[6]

Another reason that "God" has not received more attention is that some scholars believe that the NT writings essentially presuppose and take over an understanding of God from the Old Testament and the ancient Jewish setting and that there is little distinctive or notable that the NT contributes further to the topic. This is one of the factors cited by Andreas Lindemann in his analysis of Paul's statements about "God."[7] In the introduction to his study of Paul's language about God, Neil Richardson cites a comment by E. P. Sanders that illustrates this view.

> From [Paul] we learn nothing new or remarkable about God. God is a God of wrath and mercy, who seeks to save rather than to condemn, but rejection of whom leads to death. One could, to be sure, list further statements by Paul about God, but it is clear that Paul did not spend his time reflecting on the nature of the deity.[8]

It is certainly true that none of the NT authors, not even Paul, seems to have been a desk-bound theologian devoting large amounts of time to pondering in some abstract way the nature and meaning of "God." They were obviously concerned more with promoting and articulating the message of God's redemption through Jesus and the behavioral consequences of assent to this message. Moreover, there is certainly much continuity between NT statements about "God" and the Jewish and biblical background of earliest Christianity, and all the major themes that Sanders mentioned are among the things that connect the beliefs about "God" in the NT with the religious matrix from which Christian faith developed.

But does this really mean that the NT offers nothing noteworthy or distinctive about God? Put another way, is there only continuity and really nothing significantly new in the way that "God" is treated in the NT?

THIS STUDY

The place of "God" in the NT justifies more attention than some scholars seem to have thought. The following chapters address some major questions concerning NT discourse about "God." In chapter 1, I engage the question of how "God" has fared in NT scholarship since Dahl's provocative essay. We shall see that the neglect has been ameliorated somewhat but that controversies continue and that some NT texts curiously remain underinvestigated as to their treatment of "God." This review of scholarship will be particularly useful, I hope, to anyone with an interest in the state of scholarly discussion of the topic, perhaps especially fellow scholars and serious students.

In chapter 2, we consider the NT God in the context of the Roman setting of many deities and in the context of early Christian controversy over whether the Christian God is or is not the deity described in the OT. I also survey here some key emphases in discourse about "God" in the NT that indicate some noteworthy and distinctive developments in religious history. My emphasis in this chapter is that in the NT "God" represents a particular deity, not some generic abstraction, and that NT discourse about "God" presents an intriguing combination of continuity with the OT and also some distinguishing features.

The central question in chapter 3 is what impact the NT emphasis on Jesus has on NT discourse about "God." I include here something often overlooked in treatments of NT theology: a brief discussion of the significance of the place of Jesus in the devotional practices reflected in the NT, and how devotion to "God" is expressed in NT texts typically with reference to Jesus. The key question in this chapter is whether this central place of Jesus in NT discourse about "God" represents effectively a new and distinctive deity or, rather, a distinctive witness to how the OT deity is now to be understood.

Chapter 4 focuses on another major feature of NT discourse about "God": the plentiful references to the divine Spirit, and the obvious question here concerns how the Spirit functions in and has an impact on this "God" discourse. I include here also discussion of how the NT presents the relationship between the Spirit and Jesus. In this chapter as well, we will see both obvious continuity with Jewish and biblical traditions and also notable new developments in the way the divine Spirit is treated.

In the final chapter, I consider two main questions. First, I discuss the extent of diversity in NT discourse about "God," and I offer a justification for the approach taken in the preceding chapters in which I treat the NT writings collectively. The second question is what to make of the typically triadic shape of NT "God" discourse and its relationship to the subsequent developments that led to the doctrine of the Trinity.

I have chosen to organize this study as a discussion of a series of questions rather than a sequential discussion of individual NT writings. Of course, this brings the potential risk of flattening artificially the richness and diversity in these writings. But my own study of the matter has persuaded me that there is sufficient coherence in key matters about "God" in the NT to make appropriate the approach taken here. In my view, the diversity within NT "God" discourse is more one of emphasis than one of stark differences. If I have overlooked something crucial, I am sure that critical reviewers will point it out! In any case, I hope that the following chapters constitute a worthwhile contribution to the study of this important subject.[9]

James Dunn has expressed the view that "The fundamental issue for a NT biblical theology is whether the message of Jesus or the message about Jesus introduced a radical disjuncture with . . . central features of what we fairly may call Israel's biblical theology." Among what Dunn terms these "central features" is the OT emphasis on "God as One."[10] Without debating here whether this question about continuity with the OT view of "God" is the fundamental issue, I do agree that it is an important one. So, at various points in the following chapters we consider this matter particularly. As we shall see, the answer to the question of whether discourse about "God" in the NT reflects essentially continuity or any significant discontinuity and innovation is not a simple one.

I should also explain here why "God" appears in quotation marks in this book (except where the term is defined by some adjective or other phrase). I do this to try to register typographically the point that the deity to whom devotion is directed in the NT was (in that Roman setting) and is (in our setting today) a particular deity, one of a number of other possible deities or definitions of deity. In popular use today, the capitalized term "God" has come to be used as if it always has an obvious, generic, and commonly accepted meaning. But this assumption basically reflects the historical, cultural impact of Christianity, especially in Western societies. That is, when people say that they either do or do not "believe in God," they typically assume some popularized view of "God" that is an amalgam of influences from Christian theology and Western philosophy (often, however, with a minimum of acquaintance shown with Christian theology or philosophy, as in examples of the so-called "new atheism").[11] Actually, however, there is no obvious or uniform sense of the term "God." Moreover, we should beware of presuming that we know what a text is saying before we read it carefully. So, "God" (with the quotation marks) is intended to keep us aware that we are trying here to grasp how the NT texts use that term. We are trying to engage the discourse about "God" that we find in the NT writings in particular. Moreover, setting off "God" in this way is intended also to reflect the dominant NT practice of using the definite article with the Greek word *theos* when referring to the deity to whom devotion is given. The NT writers took the common Greek noun for "god," *theos*, and with the addition of the definite article sought to indicate that they were referring to a very particular deity, not to some general notion of divinity of that time.

WHY THE NEW TESTAMENT?

To turn to another obvious question, it is reasonable to ask why this book focuses on the New Testament writings. Why not a book on "God" drawing upon a broader assortment of early Christian texts? The latter sort of study would be a perfectly reasonable project, of course. But I contend that it is also equally appropriate to focus on the NT. The writings that make up the NT certainly include our earliest extant writings (commonly judged to be the uncontested letters of Paul), and these provide us our earliest glimpses of Christian discourse about "God." But also, of course, the NT as a collection comprises those early Christian writings that were successful in commending themselves sufficiently widely in early Christian circles to be treated as Scripture (some of these writings much more quickly than others, to be sure), and these writings subsequently have been treated by Christians typically as of special significance in formulating and examining their faith and religious discourse. So, both for historical and theological reasons, I contend, it is perfectly in order to concentrate on the discourse about "God" in these particular texts. Certainly, as a volume in a series on biblical theology, it is appropriate to focus on scriptural texts. I do attempt to set NT discourse about

"God" in its historical context, with some limited attention given to the larger religious environment and also to the serious diversity within early Christian circles about "God" (e.g., Marcion's firm distinction between the OT deity and his). But it would have required a much larger book and would have involved a different project to try to address in more detail the larger body of early Christian texts.[12]

THE NEW TESTAMENT AND THEREAFTER

My final comments here anticipate my final point in the concluding chapter, and this is to plead that we consider NT discourse about "God" as a subject fit for study in its own right. To be sure, as we have noted in the immediately preceding paragraphs, there is a historical connection between the NT and subsequent doctrinal developments toward the Christian doctrine of the Trinity. But, as we engage the NT texts in the following chapters, let us try simply to appreciate what they have to say about "God," insofar as possible without judging them against or reading them through later doctrinal developments. That is, let us try to allow the NT texts to have their own voice in their own terms, and let us refrain from making invidious or patronizing comparisons with those later developments in Christian doctrine. The beliefs about "God" reflected in the NT texts are historically significant and deserve to be considered on their own. Moreover, however much the later figures such as the Cappadocian Fathers may be seen as crucial for Christian theology, I propose that the NT texts may reward amply serious theological engagement with them. It may well require some cognitive adjustment on our part, however, to engage seriously the categories and themes that we find in discourse about "God" in the NT.

Furthermore, we do not have anywhere in the NT a systematic or comprehensive treatment of "God." Instead we must cope with discourse of a more occasional nature and one that is more expressive of convictions and emphases with which typically the NT authors presume acquaintance by their intended readers. But I hope that the following chapters will at least encourage readers (whether professional scholars or the wider public) that it is worth the effort to give attention to what the NT texts offer as discourse about "God."

CHAPTER ONE

"GOD" IN/AND NEW TESTAMENT SCHOLARSHIP

The immediate observation to make about how NT scholarship has treated "God" is that things have improved since Dahl published his lament, especially in the last couple of decades. There is a still-modest but somewhat increased body of scholarly publications that are either specifically focused on "God" in the NT or at least include a substantial discussion of the topic.[1] In a number of cases, it is obvious that Dahl's essay factored in helping to generate scholarly interest in the treatment of "God" in the NT, as reflected in the citation of his essay in many of these more recent publications. Even though the body of publications in question is finite, my intention here is not primarily to give an exhaustive review of them. Instead, in what follows I aim to portray the broad directions of scholarly study on "God" through considering what I hope are works sufficiently representative. Our key concerns will be to see how scholars have gone about engaging this demanding topic and what developments we see in their efforts.

For any scholarly discussion of "God" in the NT, there is the immediate question of how to organize matters. Dahl posed as alternative options either "to represent the form and function of theological language" in individual NT writings or to give "a systematic treatment of major themes" across the whole of the NT. In either case, he urged, scholars must consider both the unity and the variety in the theological emphases reflected in the NT.[2] This concern about the question of unity and diversity in the NT applies, of course, to practically any discussion of theological ideas in the NT, as is reflected in the major NT theologies of recent years (to which I return later in this discussion).[3] It is a somewhat simpler task to focus on a particular NT writer or writing, however, and it is therefore understandable that the majority of scholarly publications to be considered have this more restricted coverage. So, I begin by noting important examples of this sort.

"GOD" IN PAULINE WRITINGS

We may begin with studies of "God" in Paul's Epistles. Perhaps the earliest major work to note is Halvor Moxnes's 1980 monograph on Paul's presentation of "God" in Romans.[4] Moxnes's book, based on his PhD thesis, which was done partly under Dahl's supervision, focused particularly on Romans 1–4 and 9–11, where references to "God" are particularly frequent. His aim was to show how Paul's statements about "God" reflect issues then current, especially among fellow Christian Jews, over the status of Gentile converts and the continuing religious significance of "Israel." That is, Moxnes emphasized how Paul's God-statements must be seen in their literary and historical context. Moxnes advocated proceeding from detailed study of individual statements about "God" to assessing "the place and function of theology within Paul's thinking as a whole" and, thereafter, "the function of theology in the historical situation of Paul and his audience."

Moxnes's study reflects the sort of foundational work on which a proper theological analysis of "God" in the NT should be built, certainly. But, to use a distinction that Dahl made, what Moxnes provided was more a contribution to a history of earliest Christian beliefs about "God."[5] It is entirely right that NT theology be informed by careful studies of the history of early Christian beliefs. But NT theology and the history of early Christian beliefs are distinguishable tasks, and the one cannot substitute for the other.

In the early 1990s two further important monographs on Paul's view of "God" appeared. The key questions in Paul-Gerhard Klumbies's 1992 book were how Paul's ideas about "God" related to beliefs in Jewish tradition and in what way(s) Paul might have appropriated and altered them.[6] So, the first major portion of his discussion was a survey of references to "God" in Second Temple Jewish texts (pseudepigraphical literature, Qumran, and Jewish writers such as Philo and Josephus). Klumbies also more briefly discussed possible evidence of the beliefs about "God" that circulated in Christian "pre-Pauline tradition." Thereafter, Klumbies conducted an exegetical analysis of a body of key Pauline texts from 1 Thessalonians, 1–2 Corinthians, Philippians, and Romans, and then offered some synthesizing conclusions.

Klumbies judged that for Paul "God" was not a subject for speculation, but instead his God-statements are characteristically linked to soteriological and christological emphases. That is, "God" appears characteristically in statements about divine redemptive actions and purposes, such as God sending forth or giving over Jesus for the redemption of believers (e.g., Gal 4:4-6; Rom 8:31-33).

Also, emphasizing "the fundamental significance of christology for Pauline statements about God" and that Paul's God-talk is thoroughly shaped by his faith in Christ, Klumbies insisted that Paul's view of "God" is in a significant measure quite distinguishable from Jewish views of the time. Granting that the God about whom Paul speaks is the God of Abraham and Moses, nevertheless, Klumbies urged, Paul filled inherited statements about "God" with new content.[7] Most centrally, for Paul the key defining revelation of God was Christ instead of Torah, which represents a serious discontinuity with Jewish tradition. Indeed, Klumbies argued that the major continuity between Paul and his Jewish/OT background is a retrospective one. In the light of his perception of Jesus' significance, Paul retrospectively understood all previous references to "God" in the OT and Jewish tradition. For Paul, God was always in some sense "in Christ," and the OT is a prefiguring and anticipation of the manifestation of Christ. That is, Paul's God-talk was Christ-oriented; Christ was not simply added onto a previously fixed view of God.[8]

Klumbies contended that Paul's view of "God" is also readily distinguishable from "pre-Pauline" Christian tradition, positing that Paul placed a greater emphasis both on the meaning of Jesus' redemptive death as the uniquely significant revelation of "God" and manifestation of divine love and also on faith as the essential human response to God's redemptive actions.[9] Moreover, Klumbies urged that Paul distinctively articulated a more thoroughly christological understanding of "God" and of Christ as not only Messiah but also as the divinely ordained basis and pattern for the divine sonship of believers. In sum, granting that Paul was not an academic theologian, nevertheless Klumbies portrays him as a significant and major figure whose statements about "God" make him unique among NT writers.

Neil Richardson's 1994 monograph (based on his 1992 PhD thesis) has a related but distinguishable focus as an extended linguistic study of key Pauline passages where God-statements are particularly prominent and clustered (especially Rom 9–11; 12:1–15:7; 1 Cor 1:18–3:23; 2 Cor 2:14–4:6). After registering the Christian theological concerns that make his study important, Richardson complained about the neglect of Paul's God-language in NT scholarship, judging that "the significance of Paul's language about God has been greatly underestimated" and that there was "no overview of Paul's teaching about God."[10] Toward the end of his study, Richardson alleged a "remarkable neglect in New Testament scholarship of what the New Testament teaches about God, and the striking difference of opinion among New Testament scholars about whether a new understanding of God is indeed reflected in the writings of Paul."[11]

Richardson's key questions were "how far were Paul's concept of and language about God changed by his conversion to the Christian faith?" and also to what extent did the "ideas and language about God [shape] Paul's understanding of Christ and the language which Paul used about Christ?"[12]

On the first question, Richardson concluded that Paul's "hermeneutical standpoint" was Christ and that this meant that Paul differed from "all his non-Christian contemporaries."[13] Richardson had in mind particularly Paul's Jewish contemporaries, and he contended that Paul was also actually more theocentric than most Jewish texts of the period, which (in Richardson's view) often focused more on OT worthies such as Moses or Abraham or Israel or (as in Qumran) some elect subset of Israel than on "God." Ironically, Richardson argued, Paul's powerful experience of Christ and the consequent realization of Christ's great significance as the unique revelation of "God" produced this distinctively theocentric outlook.[14]

Richardson judged, however, that "Paul reworked traditional [Jewish/OT] God-language" and that there was "both continuity and discontinuity with the Old Testament and later Jewish language about and understanding of God."

> Paul's thought and writings are *both* theocentric *and* Christocentric; Paul's language about God and his language about Christ are so intertwined that neither can properly be understood without the other.[15]

One of the results, Richardson urged, was that for Paul "Christ *universalized and radicalized* the Old Testament understanding of the grace and love of God," transcending the focus on Israel to include all nations.[16]

Noting that not all of Paul's God-language was "distinctively Christian" but was heavily indebted to his Jewish background, nevertheless, Richardson concluded, "much of it is implicitly christological," and there is a "vital interdependence of language about God and language about Christ" in Paul. Yet Richardson also posited that Paul's Christ-language is "grammatically subordinate" to his God-language, which "points to God as origin, author, warrant and goal," Christ characteristically referred to as the unique agent of divine purposes.[17] This produces a paradoxical conclusion. On the one hand, Paul's thought is "deeply theocentric," and "time and again God is emphatically the ultimate reference-point." On the other hand, "much of his God-language alternates with, and is even dependent on, language about Christ."[18] In sum, "If it is true that Paul uses God-language in order to interpret and 'define' Christ, it is also true that language about Christ in turn redefines the identity of God."[19]

One of the works cited by Richardson is Larry Kreitzer's 1987 study, *Jesus and God in Paul's Eschatology*. This is another noteworthy contribution to scholarly studies of Paul's thought, but the focus is limited to the ways that Paul links Jesus and God in his statements expressive of eschatological expectations and hopes.[20] Kreitzer refers to a Pauline "transference" or shift of terms and roles from God to Christ, but Richardson (rightly in my view) judged that it is more accurate to characterize Paul's thought as involving an "overlap" in which Christ shares in some of God's attributes and actions.[21] That is, we may think of Paul as reflecting a unique and remarkable inclusion of Jesus into roles, attributes, and significance otherwise reserved for "God" in biblical/Jewish tradition.

Even though it is restricted to an examination of key Pauline passages, Richardson's book is probably the fullest study of Paul's references to "God" and presents a generally balanced and nuanced discussion. It combines careful exegesis that includes detailed linguistic analysis of Pauline statements about "God" with explicit theological concern. We may note a further interesting observation registered by Richardson. Although he agreed that we must avoid reading later doctrinal developments back into New Testament texts, Richardson contended that there is no great discontinuity between Paul and the later theological developments of the patristic period. Certainly, he granted, the one is not the other.

> Yet Paul's emphasis on the lordship of Christ as the new and final expression of Jewish monotheism, the incarnational implications of much of his language about Christ, together with the explication of his

God-language by its association with Christ-language and Spirit-language, suggest that the later doctrines of the Incarnation and Trinity were the logical consequences of his theological grammar.[22]

This is likely a view to which some others, but not all, would give unqualified assent. I noted earlier Richardson's reference to a continuing difference of opinion among scholars about whether Paul's view of "God" represents a distinctively Christian reshaping of Jewish beliefs in the light of christological convictions or whether Paul essentially took over a view of God from Jewish tradition and simply added onto it beliefs about Jesus. In some other contributions to the study of Paul's theology we see this difference of opinion vividly.

Gordon Fee's massive study of Paul's references to the Spirit of God constitutes a forceful assertion that Paul operated with "thoroughly Trinitarian presuppositions," for "not only has the coming of Christ changed everything for Paul, so too has the coming of the Spirit."[23] In Fee's analysis, Paul operated with a "Trinitarian understanding of God" that was "foundational to the heart of his theological enterprise—*salvation in Christ*."[24] To cite Fee's own forthright statement:

> Salvation is God's activity, from beginning to end: God the Father initiated it, in that it belongs to God's eternal purposes (1 Cor 2:6-9), has its origins in God and has God as its ultimate goal (1 Cor 8:6), and was set in motion by his having sent both the Son and the Spirit (Gal 4:4-7). Christ the Son effected eschatological salvation for the people of God through his death and resurrection, the central feature of all Pauline theology. The effectual realization and appropriation of the love of God as offered by the Son is singularly the work of the Spirit. . . . There is no salvation in Christ which is not fully Trinitarian in this sense.[25]

In his large study of Paul's theology (1998), however, James Dunn strikes a somewhat different emphasis.[26] Dunn freely acknowledges "how fundamental to Paul's theology was the experience of his conversion" and "the extent to which Christ is bound up with Paul's sense of personal knowledge of and relationship with God."[27] Early in his chapter on "God," he notes that the "God-given 'revelation of Christ' did not leave his fundamental belief in God unaffected."[28] But in Dunn's comparatively brief discussion of Paul's beliefs about "God," the dominant emphasis is that "Paul's convictions about God are all too axiomatic" and were

"Jewish through and through," e.g., God as "one," as the creator, and as especially linked to the history of Israel.[29] So, Dunn contends, there is little elaboration of beliefs about "God" in Paul, for "they were already common to and shared with his readers." Moreover, Dunn states that Paul's "'speech about God' was part of the shared speech of the first Christian congregations, already a fundamental 'taken-for-granted' of their common discourse."[30]

So, Dunn devotes only 23 pages to "God," whereas the largest chapter of Dunn's weighty tome is devoted to Paul's beliefs about Jesus, comprising some 152 pages, and in his final chapter Dunn devotes a further section to Christ as "the fulcrum point of Paul's theology."[31] In this latter discussion, Dunn certainly makes much of Jesus' significance for Paul. Thus, e.g., Dunn says that "Christ was the decisive factor," playing the "pivotal role" in Paul's theology, "the central criterion by which Paul made critical discrimination of what counted and what was of lesser moment." Moreover, Dunn writes of the "realignment" of Paul's Jewish heritage, stating that "in Paul's theology Christ gave that heritage clearer definition." Indeed, Dunn judges, "For Paul, God was now to be known definitively by reference to Christ," God's character revealed "most fully in terms of Christ" such that "the revelation of Christ was the revelation of God," the result being that "Christ became the definition of God."[32]

Nevertheless, it seems significant that Dunn thereafter also registers some puzzlement that Paul's gospel required that "faith had to be in Christ and could no longer be simply in God," for in Dunn's view Paul "never properly explains" this. Indeed, Dunn adds, "Presumably he could have envisaged a saving faith which was not focused in Christ as such."[33]

I have to say that I find Dunn's statements here somewhat curious. The reason for the essential place of Jesus as object of faith for Paul is surely that he believed that God sent forth his Son to be the eschatological agent of redemption, and in light of this divine action in Jesus the only appropriate human response is grateful acknowledgement and confession of it. For Paul, faith that ignores Jesus would be a disobedient or ignorant faith, not because Paul was simply narrow in mind-set but because for him faith was always to be shaped in response to God's revelatory actions, of which Jesus is the climactic one.

A somewhat similar (and more sharply worded) response to Dunn's discussion of Paul's view of "God" was lodged by Francis Watson.[34] Although he characterizes Dunn's *Theology of Paul* as "the culmination of the most significant project in Pauline interpretation of the later twentieth century," Watson contends that Dunn's representation of Paul's view of "God" is "symptomatic of a mis-reading so fundamental as to distort out of all recognition the basic shape of Pauline theology."[35] Watson claims that Dunn's concern to emphasize continuity of Paul with his Jewish heritage operates at the expense of seeing how profoundly for Paul Christ resignifies "God" and redefines valid faith in God. Watson urges, "Paul's texts everywhere assert or assume a distinctively Christian view of God," and "traditional Jewish God-language is relocated within a framework in which the word 'God' is misunderstood and misused if it is not always and everywhere accompanied by reference to Jesus and to his Spirit."[36]

In a section of his article entitled "The Deity of God is Inseparable from the Agency of God," Watson emphasizes how God's acts comprised for Paul the basis of his view of "God" and of faith: "For Paul, God is 'the one who raised Jesus our Lord from the death' (Rom 4.24; 8.11), and the raising of Jesus discloses not only what God does but, at the same time, who God is."[37] Paul's emphasis on "the obligatory nature of faith in Christ" is not some arbitrary legal demand imposed by God; instead, it flows from Paul's understanding of valid faith now as properly "the human acknowledgement and confession of the prior divine action in Christ, and of the divine being disclosed and constituted in this action."[38] For Paul, the faith of Abraham was "the anticipatory form of acknowledgement of the divine *promise*," and so Abraham's faith was "oriented towards the event in which Jesus is handed over for our trespasses and raised for our justification (Rom 4.25)." Thus, for Paul there was no tension between a "theocentric" faith and faith centered on Christ.[39] In sum, Watson contends, for Paul "God is who God is only in relation to Jesus, and conversely Jesus is who he is only in relation to God."[40] That is, in light of God's sending forth of his Son, "Jesus is integral to God's own identity."[41]

Watson's critique of Dunn extends still further, however, to Dunn's treatment of the Spirit in Paul.[42] Watson alleges that Dunn does not adequately reflect how much for Paul "the Spirit is the Spirit of the *risen* Jesus," the role of the Spirit being "*to enable participation in the life that the crucified and risen Jesus shares with the God he addresses as 'Abba, Father', who appointed him as his Son in the act of raising him from the dead.*"[43] Watson urges that Paul's references to the Spirit must be seen in connection with what he says about God and Jesus so that "the coherence and the soteriological relevance of Paul's trinitarian God-language will be brought to light."[44] In short, Watson seems to take a view of Paul's theology that is very close to that urged by Richardson, even echoing Fee in characterizing Paul as "trinitarian."

We should also note the large article on "God" in the *Dictionary of Paul and His Letters*, cowritten by Donald Guthrie and Ralph P. Martin.[45] The article is a workmanlike discussion of NT references to "God," covering "Basic Assumptions" (largely beliefs taken over from Paul's Jewish heritage), "God as Creator, Father and King," God's "Attributes" (God's glory, wisdom and knowledge, holiness, righteousness and justice, love and mercy, goodness and faithfulness, uniqueness), and God's "Unity." As should be clear even from this brief description, the article essentially reflects fairly traditional categories for describing "God" in theological circles. It is, of course, a difficult task to deal adequately with such a huge topic within a restricted space, even within such a large article. But one gets the impression that the authors have gone for fitting Pauline evidence within a more generic theological framework, which has the unfortunate effect of suppressing somewhat the contours and main features of Paul's view of "God."

For example, it is only in the subsection on "The Unity of God" toward the end of the article that we get a discussion of how Jesus figured in Paul's view of "God." The authors grant that the emergence of the Christian gospel constituted "an entirely new factor" and that we see a remarkable accommodation of the risen Jesus into Paul's inherited Jewish view of God, "now broadened and deepened to make space for the exalted Lord who in worship was greeted as on a par with Yahweh and worthy of divine honors and praise."[46] The phenomena reflecting the enlargement of Paul's Jewish monotheism represent "adumbrations of the Trinity." Yet the affirmations of the "divine nature of both Jesus Christ and the Spirit" attested in Paul did not mean postulating three gods: "The conviction that God was active in Christ and in the Spirit prevented this from happening."[47] About the Spirit, however, the authors have little to say, other than a few passing references.

In short, the article focuses on traditional theological attributes and does less than justice to the more dynamic nature of Paul's references to "God." Surely, any discussion of Paul's view of "God" that treats Jesus almost as an add-on feature and that fails to give any focused attention to the Spirit must be judged something of a disappointment.

"GOD" IN THE GOSPELS

The Gospels are the other NT texts that have received significant scholarly attention as to how they present "God."[48] All four canonical Gospels have been addressed by scholars, but it appears that GMark and GJohn have received somewhat more attention than the others, with GMatthew receiving the least attention. The narrative genre of these writings has meant that studies have sometimes involved more of an analysis of the "role" of "God" as a character in the Jesus story, employing literary-critical approaches.

John Donahue's 1982 essay focused on "God" in GMark with the explicit aim of addressing the wider neglect of the topic that Dahl had identified.[49] After a brief comparison with other NT authors, Donahue proposes that GMark's references to "God" convey some distinguishable emphases (e.g., an avoidance of anthropomorphism) that suggest a certain concern to engage the wider Hellenistic world with an evangelistic intent.[50] Noting that the explicit Markan references to "God" are mainly in sayings of Jesus, Donahue concentrated attention on three pericopes in Mark 12:13-34 where Jesus makes statements about God. The net effect, Donahue argues, is that in these passages Jesus is pictured as articulating a view of God that seems somewhat related to the lofty views reflected in such texts as *Wisdom of Solomon*. Yet also, of course, the Markan narrative presents Jesus as the unique agent of God's power and purposes, reflecting the profound convictions about Jesus' significance that obviously are the major concern of the Gospel.

A couple of German-language essays in the 1990s made forays into the subject. François Vouga focused on the Markan emphasis on faith in God and on Jesus as herald of God's kingdom, arguing that Jesus' summons to discipleship reflects the OT prophetic tradition. In short, Vouga argued for a strongly functional Christology thoroughly subordinated to an emphasis on "God."[51] Klaus Scholtissek's 1996 essay traced usage of the term "God" in GMark yielding main themes: "God" as the God of Israel, the creator-deity, the one God whose kingdom brings salvation. Scholtissek concluded that Mark is theocentric in that Jesus operates in fulfillment of God's will, and Markan discipleship is obedience to God.[52]

Paul Danove's 2001 article presented a linguistic analysis of nearly 200 "explicit and grammatically required implicit references to God in Mark 1:1–16:8" and their distribution in GMark's narrative.[53] Danove contended that in Mark 1:1-15 we have the greatest relative frequency of reference to "God" of any passage in GMark, with "seventeen points of information about God."[54] He then observed "the direct or indirect insinuation of Jesus into every aspect of the characterization of God in 1:1-15," which establishes a strong bond between Jesus and God as characters in the narrative "that precludes any understanding of either character without immediate reference to the other."[55] Indeed, Danove assessed the narrative function of "God" in GMark along the same lines.

> Within Mark, the characterization of God is placed in the service of establishing and redundantly reinforcing the credentials of Jesus, encouraging the readers' identification with Jesus, especially in his suffering and death, and inviting the reader to a deeper relationship with God grounded in the knowledge that this relationship demands fidelity unto death.[56]

Soon after Danove's article came Jack Kingsbury's contribution to the *Festschrift* for Paul Achtemeier.[57] Kingsbury focused on the "point of view" of the Markan narrative and contended that the Markan author effectively presents "the whole of his gospel story from the point of view of God."[58] Somewhat similarly to Danove, Kingsbury judged that the author's main aim was to present Jesus as bearing full divine approval as "anointed royal son" explicitly acknowledged by God and the one through whom God brings eschatological salvation.[59] That is, "God" functions in GMark essentially to identify and endorse Jesus and also as the origin and ultimate meaning for Jesus' activities.

Drew Smith's 2002 substantial article gave an analysis of GMark's Christology as an aspect of the narrative's *theology*, Smith arguing that "Mark's Christology is better understood within the framework of Mark's theology."[60] Smith examined successively GMark's presentation of Jesus as sent from God, "actor for God" (Jesus' miracles as expressions of God's authority, the defeat of God's enemies, God's compassion and comfort, and God's "numinous presence"), and the one who speaks for God. In a dialectical statement expressing a conclusion similar to Danove and Kingsbury, Smith concluded that "as God is presented in the narrative as the authenticator of Jesus, so Jesus is presented as the authoritative actor and speaker for God."[61] But Smith perhaps goes a step further in judging that "God plays the main role in the narrative, being the sender, authenticator, commissioner, and vindicator of Jesus" and that "the significance and identify of Jesus in Mark is an aspect of the narrative presentation of God."[62]

19

To date, the only published monograph-length study of "God" in GMark is Guttenberger's large 2004 volume.[63] Guttenberger discusses the Markan view of "God" under five main headings: God as Lord of history, God as lawgiver, God as powerful/almighty, God and evil, and God's uniqueness in relationship to Christology. She argues that GMark presents God as creator and the giver of Torah; but Jesus now supersedes Moses as the authoritative interpreter of God's will, thereby also effectively superseding Torah itself.[64] Some of her conclusions are controversial, e.g., her view that GMark portrays God as making temporary space for evil and opposition and that Jesus' crucifixion is thus purely a negative event.[65] Also controversial are her claims that the motif of silencing demonic acclamation reflects a concern to avoid any claim by Jews that Jesus' high status creates a conflict with monotheism[66] or that "God" in GMark is presented as distanced from the world and history.[67] I think also that GMark should be seen as more upbeat than her characterization (although she is by no means alone in ascribing to GMark a dark and almost existentialist outlook!). But hers is the major study of "God" in Mark with which any subsequent investigation must interact.

It is curious that to date there seems to be no extended study of "God" in GMatthew. There is Mowery's 1988 modest essay, which surveyed the references to God as "Father" in GMatthew, but little else to report.[68] This curious neglect of GMatthew is reflected in the absence of a treatment of it in the Achtemeier *Festschrift*, which otherwise provides rather wide coverage of "God" in the New Testament.[69]

As Mowery noted, GMatthew uses "Father" for God far more frequently than any other of the Synoptics (44 times), nearly as often as GMatthew's use of *Theos*.[70] "Father" as a term for God appears only in sayings of Jesus, the majority of instances (typically "your/our heavenly Father," e.g., 5:16, 45; 6:1, 9) in passages where Jesus gives directions and assurances of various sorts (seventeen instances in the Sermon on the Mount). In some cases, GMatthew has "Father" in sayings where GMark has "*Theos*" (cf. Matt 12:50/Mark 3:35; Matt 26:29/Mark 14:25), and similarly in Q material GMatthew shows a greater fondness for "Father" than GLuke (cf. Matt 5:45/Luke 6:35; Matt 6:26/Luke 12:24; Matt 10:29-32/Luke 12:6-8). In addition, GMatthew has a larger body of references to "God" in Jesus' sayings, which emphasize God's all-seeing, all-knowing faithfulness, some of these sayings unique to GMatthew (e.g., 6:1-8). So, it appears that there is ample material for a full-scale study of "God" in GMatthew.

For GLuke-Acts there is a somewhat larger body of scholarly work published. Brawley's 1990 volume focused on "God" in GLuke-Acts as a case study for an introduction to a particular kind of sophisticated narrative analysis and seems as much (or more) concerned with the latter task as it is with discussing "God."[71]

John Carroll approached GLuke-Acts as texts that were frequently read and pondered in early Christian circles, seeking to develop "a picture that would result from repeated reading, or hearing, of the narrative over a period of time."[72] Carroll noted that references to God as "Father" are in Jesus' sayings and so almost entirely appear only in GLuke. He also traced themes in the Luke-Acts presentation of "God," e.g., God as Savior of Israel and the world.

Diane Chen's more recent volume traces a continuity in the portrayal of "God" in GLuke-Acts and in biblical and Second Temple Jewish traditions, and Chen contends that GLuke-Acts emphasizes God as a merciful, faithful, and authoritative "Father." She notes how GLuke-Acts explicitly presents God as fulfilling OT promises in Jesus, and she also observes interesting similarities between the Lukan emphases on God as "Father" and the Augustan claims of the emperor as *pater patriae*.[73]

"God" in the Gospel of John has received attention from several scholars, including Barrett's 1982 study on the place of "God" in the Johannine presentation of strong claims about Jesus.[74] Paul Meyer produced a sensitive probing of how in GJohn "christology" concerns "first, foremost, and always—[Jesus'] open or hidden relationship to God, and of God to him."[75] Still more recently, Francis Moloney judged that GJohn's story of Jesus relates how "God has entered history in and through the person of Jesus."[76]

Tord Larsson's novel study combines a detailed review of six major scholars' work on GJohn across several centuries (Luther, Calvin, Westcott, Holtzmann, Bultmann, and Raymond Brown) with Larsson's own analysis of "God" in GJohn. Larsson posits some interesting continuities among these scholars and emphasizes the multifaceted presentation and role of "God" in GJohn, arguing that this writing is one of the most important influences that shaped the classic Christian notion of "God."[77]

But, unquestionably, the most important recent study of "God" in GJohn is Marianne Meye Thompson's 2001 volume.[78] Concurring with several previous scholars that " 'Christocentric' is a misleading term for the Gospel of John" and that the Christology of GJohn can be grasped properly only in the larger context of the Johannine treatment of *theology*, she focuses on "the identity of God in the Fourth Gospel."[79]

To cite only a few of her many valuable judgments, Thompson rightly observes that in GJohn Jesus' significance is articulated entirely with reference to God "the Father," and "God" is identified emphatically with Jesus. To be sure, "God" is the deity of the biblical tradition but "is identified most characteristically in relationship to Jesus, rather than in relationship to any of the patriarchs, heroes of the faith, or the people of Israel." Indeed, "terms for God, as well as the entire understanding of God, must now be delineated with respect to Jesus."[80]

Yet she also rightly notes that "it is the failure to make the theological correlates of Christology explicit that has led to neglect of the figure of God in NT theology."[81] That is, although GJohn and the rest of the NT foreground the significance of Jesus, this significance is essentially stated in terms of Jesus' role and status as the one in and through whom God is revealed in a unique and climactic way.[82]

STUDIES OF "GOD" IN THE NT

In the period under review, there have also been a number of studies on "God" in the NT more broadly. Here again, limitations of space require that I highlight key studies instead of attempting exhaustive coverage.[83]

According to James Reese's quantitative analysis of the 421 statements about "God" that he identified in the NT, the overwhelmingly most frequent type of statement refers to God as "Father": 183 such statements (43 percent) distributed across every NT writing except 3 John, the largest number of these in GJohn (86 of 133 "God" statements), followed by GMatthew (23 of 41 statements).[84] Reese judged that the bulk of the remaining 238 statements in his list present "God" using a small cluster of images/themes, the most frequent being "the image of the God of salvation history" (111 statements in 14 NT writings, of which 40 are in GJohn).[85] Of these, the key divine act singled out for special treatment is the resurrection of Jesus: 84 statements in 13 NT writings.

Reese's brief study is heuristically useful in its analytical approach, but I think that he oversimplifies matters in saying that "the centrality of Jesus [in the NT] pushes the role of God into the background."[86] It seems more accurate to say that the NT foregrounds Jesus solely as the agent of "God's" purposes.

Neil Richardson's modest 1999 volume offers a threefold approach to the NT involving linguistic analysis of the language used for "God," a description of the "imprint of God" on people in the NT, especially Jesus and Paul, and a synthesizing study of how NT authors relate to one another.[87] Richardson contends that "the New Testament has more to say about God than about any other subject except Jesus," and so he found it surprising that so little had been written on the subject. One of his main concerns, which he judged to be rarely addressed, was "whether the New Testament's claim of a new revelation of God . . . carries with it a new understanding of God."[88] That is, the NT reflects both continuity and discontinuity with the OT in its presentation of "God," but of what does the discontinuity consist?

Richardson's conclusion was that the newness and discontinuity of the NT's presentation of "God" constitutes something substantial: "God is now defined, so to speak, not as the God who brought Israel up out of Egypt, although that remained true, but as the God who raised Jesus from the dead."[89] Moreover, Richardson contended that Paul's view of the programmatic incorporation of Gentiles into the elect meant that "the language of particularity applied to God is, for Paul, at an end," this representing "one of the clearest examples of discontinuity between the old and the new understandings of God."[90]

But is this so? Is the NT emphasis on the unique significance of Jesus and faith in Jesus as defining the circle of the elect any less particularistic than the OT emphasis on Israel as God's people? It seems to me that it would be better to say that in the NT the particularity of God remains but is relocated in Jesus.

In a brief but incisive article published in the same year as Richardson's book, Christfried Böttrich focused on key affirmations about "God" in the NT, particularly God as "Father," "one," various epithets indicating God's universal and surpassing status (e.g., "most High," "Lord of heaven and earth"), God's raising of Jesus from death, and several other epithets.[91] Contrary to some assertions, Böttrich (rightly in my view) concluded that in the NT "God" consistently plays an active role and that in this the NT authors stand "in unbroken continuity with the faith-tradition of Israel."[92]

To jump ahead chronologically to one of the latest publications considered here, Christiane Zimmermann's massive 2007 volume presents a greatly expanded study basically along the lines of Böttrich's article.[93] This is an astonishingly wide-ranging and extensive study of all the prominent types of affirmations about "God" in the NT (e.g., "Father," creator, various terms indicating "God's" status as lord and master, "God" as life giver, one/only God, "most high") and a good many of the less frequent ones as well. In her discussion of "God" as life giving, there is a special extended section on NT references to "God" as having resurrected Jesus. In addition to the sheer extent of its coverage, Zimmermann's book also offers thoughtful summarizing conclusions, such as her observations about how OT/Jewish traditions about "God" as "Father" are taken over and given more pronounced emphasis in the NT in the focus on Jesus as "God's" unique Son and Christian believers as "God's" family. I also note her observation that OT/Jewish tradition about "God" as life-giving takes on a new and distinctive role in the emphasis that "God" raised Jesus from death. Zimmermann's hefty tome will simply be required reading for any further scholarly investigation of what the NT says about "God."

Marianne Meye Thompson's monograph on the NT depiction of "God" as "Father," though smaller in size and coverage (with a focus on the Gospels and Paul), is nevertheless a noteworthy contribution that also was prompted by issues arising from feminist critique of the NT and traditional Christian confession of "God" as "Father."[94] One of the significant features of her study is a careful and balanced assessment of Joachim Jeremias's claims about Jesus' use of *Abba* as prayer-address for "God," with Thompson concluding that Jesus did likely use the expression but that this reflects more continuity with ancient Jewish piety than Jeremias recognized.[95] Indeed, in general Thompson argues that Jesus and the NT stand in closer continuity with the OT and ancient Jewish piety than is sometimes realized.

This forms part of her larger argument that NT references to "God" as "Father" must be understood as part of a "trajectory" that has "its starting point in the Old Testament and the relationship of 'God' to the people of Israel," and that "aims at an eschatological horizon, when God's promises to all the people of God are ultimately fulfilled and they enjoy that relationship of trust and love signified by calling upon God as Father." Thompson insists that the NT designation of "God" as "Father" reflects both a christological and an ecclesiological emphasis: "God" as "Father" of "the Son" and "Father of a people."[96] She also insists that this "eschatological trajectory of God's Fatherhood" (which she traces through OT and Second Temple Jewish sources on into the NT and further into the eschatological horizon) both preserves the unavoidable particularity of biblical teaching about "God" and also provides a basis for affirming

"God" as "Father" without privileging maleness or making the biblical God simply a projection of patriarchal values.[97] Essentially, she argues, "God" is rightly addressed by Christians as "Father" as an expression of indebtedness and alignment with this God's historic revelations to Israel and in Jesus, in which the image of "God" as "Father" functioned to reflect particularly this God's "redemptive and life-giving work."[98]

Jerome Neyrey's 2004 volume, *Render to God*, is an analysis of eight NT writings (GMark, GMatthew, GJohn, Acts, Romans, 1 Corinthians, Galatians, Hebrews), with a social-scientific orientation focusing on such categories as "client/patron" relationships.[99] The results seem to be a bit heavily shaped by the desire to fit NT writings into such categories. For example, is it really illuminating, or even really accurate, to portray Jesus as God's "client" in GMark and to posit a shift in representation of Jesus from "client" to "co-patron" with "God" by the book of Hebrews? Is Jesus any less human and "God's" agent of redemption in Hebrews than in GMark; and is Jesus really any less uniquely "God's" Son in GMark than in Hebrews?[100]

CONCLUSIONS

As we near the end of this review of scholarship on the topic, one obvious conclusion is that Dahl's complaint about the neglect of "God" in NT studies was noticed and that a number of scholars have sought to address that neglect in the years since his oft-cited essay. Recent reference works include articles not noted in this review that further reflect a redress of the alleged neglect.[101] Most recently, there is the discussion of "The Theology of God" by Dunn in his *New Testament Theology*, a volume in the series to which the present study forms a contribution.[102] But if "God" is no longer an ignored "stepchild" in NT scholarship, what further conclusions can we draw from the body of work surveyed?[103]

Clearly, most of these studies have dealt with particular NT writers/writings. This may reflect an appropriately finite and focused outlook, of course. But I wonder if it also reflects the highly (over?) specialized nature of NT scholarship, and perhaps even a certain hesitation about whether the NT represents a sufficiently cohesive religious stance that it can be treated holistically. NT scholars are all well aware that there are variations in emphases, and in some matters even more serious occasional differences, among the NT writings. Consequently, for some time now it has been fashionable to emphasize variation, perhaps at the expense of registering what may unite the NT. Indeed, I think that we must suppose some significant amount of congruence (or at least perceived congruence) among these writings for them to have made their way into the emerging Christian canon in the early centuries.

If we turn to the recent studies that attempt to treat "God" more broadly across the NT, questions about how to register the diversity and coherence of these writings are evident. So, most of these works address a selection of writers/writings, typically a chapter on each one included in the study, and usually a concluding chapter in which the author may summarize distinctions among the writings considered and/or may attempt to identify some connections. It appears that a concern to represent the diversity and distinguishing features of NT writers/writings is a major factor, and one could ask whether the representation of NT coherence in "God" is weak in comparison. I wonder also whether we scholars are too readily content with a description of NT ideas of "God" without probing more deeply the theological convictions involved.

Scholarly analysis of "God" in the NT has other problems too, including how to identify relevant evidence to consider. On the one hand, "God" does not receive extended foreground discussion anywhere in the NT, and yet the entire body of NT writings presupposes and reflects beliefs about who "God" is and what "God" has done, and these beliefs are arguably central and critical in every one of these writings. So how should one treat such a topic that is so pervasive across the NT and yet not readily available in handy defined passages? Is it the case that "God" is more a presupposition of the NT and not really a topic on which there is much concern to comment in these writings? Is the concern to articulate Jesus' significance so great that "God" is nearly eclipsed?

Certainly, this body of scholarship attests commendable efforts to engage the overlooked topic of "God" in the NT, and a number of these studies comprise noteworthy contributions to our perception of how "God" is treated in various NT writings/writers. But there are important NT writings that have not yet had the attention that they deserve relating to "God," including some major NT writings (e.g., GMatthew, Revelation, Hebrews). Also, I reiterate the observation that these studies are (with a few exceptions) heavily descriptive, and that there is considerable room for further analysis and reflection on the God witnessed to in the NT.

CHAPTER TWO

WHO IS "GOD" IN THE NEW TESTAMENT?

GODS GALORE

Many people, especially those living in the modern Western societies, likely regard the word *god/God* as relatively univocal and unproblematic in meaning, whatever they may think of the warrants for theistic beliefs. Influenced by centuries of Christianity, popular use of "God" usually designates, in more formal terms, "the supernatural creator and overseer of the universe," and an implicitly monotheistic assumption frames how this "God" is seen.[1] Consequently, statements such as "I do/don't believe in God" typically presuppose such a presumed generic meaning of "God," and the speaker usually assumes that the only question to consider is belief or disbelief in this established sense of the referent of the word. In short, what the word "God" means is widely taken as relatively fixed and obvious and is not an issue.

But in the ancient world of the first Christians (and in large parts of the current world as well), the words for *god* (e.g., the Greek word *theos*) designated one of many kinds of divine beings.[2] There was neither one deity nor even one genus or definition of deity. Instead, there was a veritable cafeteria of divine beings of various orders, attributes, and functions. Not only the Roman Empire as a whole but also individual nations and peoples were rather richly supplied with deities. So, in that setting, when one spoke of a "god" it was not automatically clear who or what the referent was. It could be one of the numerous traditional deities of the many cities or various peoples, or it could be new or imported ones.

Indeed, in a number of settings one could even refer to the ruler as a "god."

Moreover, the common view was that all deities were entitled to receive appropriate worship. A city or a people might well have their particular patron-deity—and might well have thought of one deity as holding pre-eminence among the gods—to whom a city or people might give special reverence. But it was understood that other cities and peoples had their deities too and that they were just as worthy of worship. Indeed, when people traveled to another city or country, ordinarily they would freely participate in the worship of the local deities, if invited, with no sense of unfaithfulness to their own deities. To be sure, philosophers of the day sometimes urged the idea that there was really one deity behind or above all the particular traditional deities, the latter sometimes thought of as manifestations of the one deity. But even those proposing such a view (sometimes referred to by scholars today as a "pagan monotheism") did not really question giving worship to all the many deities of the religious environment.[3] That is, their philosophical musings in general had little impact on popular religious behavior, not even their own.

Along with devout Jews, however, earliest Christians typically distinguished themselves in taking a rather critical stance against devotion to the many deities of the time, insisting that there was only one true and living "God" to whom alone worship was rightfully due.[4] To be sure, early Christians (and their Jewish contemporaries) conceived of a diversity of spiritual and heavenly beings, some of whom they regarded very positively, typically as part of the entourage of the one God (e.g., angels). The "monotheism" of ancient Christians and Jews was not primarily or typically expressed as a denial of the *existence* of any heavenly (or even divine) being other than the one God. Instead, their emphasis was that only the one God was the rightful recipient of worship, whether from them or from anyone else. That is, they believed that the one God held a universal right to exclusive worship and that the religious devotion offered to any other deity was an offense against the one God—"idolatry," at best a tragic expression of ignorance and at worst the gravest of sins.

We see this critical stance reflected in passages such as 1 Corinthians 8:1-6, where Paul rather clearly distinguishes between the polytheistic outlook of the larger culture and what he regards as the proper attitude of Christians for whom there is rightly only "one God, the Father" and "one Lord, Jesus Christ" to whom alone believers owe their reverence. This passage indicates that, in Paul's eyes, to offer worship to any of the many "so-called gods in heaven or on earth" (8:5 NRSV) is to engage in "idolatry" (*eidōlothytōn*, 8:1).

To cite just one more example, there is Paul's brief characterization of his Thessalonian Gentile converts as having "turned to God [*ton theon*] from idols, to serve a living and true God, and to wait for his son from heaven" (1 Thess 1:9-10 NRSV). The starkly counterposed options are clearly reflected also in this passage. On the one hand, there are the traditional deities, which Paul dismissively refers to as "idols" from which his converts have turned as part of their acceptance of the gospel, and on the other hand, the one valid deity, whom Paul identifies here as the living God who also raised Jesus from death.

These two passages are by no means unique in reflecting the religious stance advocated in the NT. They may have a particular significance, however, in that they are from the uncontested letters of Paul that must, therefore, date from ca. 50–60 C.E., well within the very first generation of the Christian movement. Moreover, it is also noteworthy that these letters are addressed to Gentile Christians living in cities where the traditional plurality of deities was the dominating feature of the religious environment. There was clearly no mincing about on Paul's part in how he sought to steer his converts' attitudes toward these deities! His language reflects a sharp polarization between the true God and the many other beings treated as gods at the time.

The passage in 1 Corinthians 8:1-6 leads into an extended Pauline response to questions from the Corinthian church about how believers should now conduct themselves in their polytheistic urban setting, constituting 1 Corinthians 8–10.[5] In some things, Paul urges a certain flexibility, e.g., in freely eating meat purchased in the market without worrying about whether it came from a sacrifice in some pagan temple and in accepting invitations to dine with nonbelieving Gentiles so long as they do not make the meal overtly in honor of a pagan deity (10:23-30). This flexibility has firm limits, however, as is especially clear in 10:1-22. Here, Paul strongly warns against participating in the worship of the pagan deities, which he calls "idolatry" (v. 14) and the sacrifices as offered to "demons" (vv. 19-21).

All of this means that the "God" of the NT is posited, not as one among others, or as one member of a divine genus, but as *sui generis*, unique and solely worthy of worship. In the NT, "God" (*ho theos*) represents something categorically distinguished from the many deities of the

Roman environment. Indeed, as illustrated by the Pauline passages that we have considered, all the other gods are to be regarded as invalid, spurious, and unworthy of worship. They are "idols" (*eidōlon*), a term with a distinctly pejorative connotation that emerged in ancient Jewish tradition and was appropriated also among earliest Christians.[6] In short, faith in the NT "God" requires a practical kind of *disbelief* in all other gods, or at least a radically negative and pejorative view of them and the worship given to them. I return to explore this matter a bit further in the concluding chapter.

Moreover, faithful commitment to "God" in the NT requires abandonment and refusal to participate in the worship of any other deity. This meant Christians absenting themselves from a variety of corporate occasions of religious ritual, for religion pervaded the social and political scenes. So, conscientious Christian practice could amount to a significant severing of believers from the pervasive religious activities of the Roman world, which could entail serious tensions with family members, neighbors, friends and associates in business or employment, and also even with civic and political authorities.[7] Elizabeth Castelli vividly captured the political significance of religious ritual in the Roman setting:

> Sacrifice keeps the tenuous balance between the human world and the divine realm intact, assures that the dramatic vagaries of divine dissatisfaction will be held in check. In the Roman context, where sacrifice serves as a first line of defense in the preservation of political stability, the refusal to sacrifice or the perversion of the carefully balanced sacrificial relations produces threatening seismic fissures running underneath the foundations of society.[8]

The pervasively public nature of religion meant that Christian withdrawal from ritual events could not readily be hidden. Faith in "God" in the NT was by no means simply a particular devotion to this deity or a belief that one held as a private religious opinion. The uniqueness of the NT "God" was to be matched by an exclusivity in the devotional behavior of believers. Their devotion to "God" required believers to disassociate or distance themselves from core activities of their cultures, especially the worship of the gods on whom the welfare of city and empire was thought to depend. That is, faith in the NT God involved both a "cognitive dissonance," believers tacitly or explicitly denying the validity of all other deities, and also an unavoidable social dissonance (which could, and as time went on, did involve sometimes severe dissonance with political authorities). As noted already, philosophers of the time toyed with various ideas about the gods with impunity (e.g., whether they were all one or whether some of them had been invented) in the cosy and safe settings of their elite circles.[9] These were little more than thought experiments with little substance and of no major impact on the religious practice of these philosophers or of people more widely. Early Christian faith in "God," however, involved a much more robust "atheism" in beliefs and religious practice![10]

"GOD" AND BIBLICAL/JEWISH TRADITION

Of course, this pugnacious attitude and the accompanying dissonant religious practice had not originated with Christians but were features inherited from the Jewish religious matrix of the Christian movement. The first believers in Jesus were Jews, and their Christian faith did not involve (in their minds at least) a conversion from their essential religious commitment to the one God witnessed to in the biblical texts and ancient Jewish tradition. Instead, as is patently clear in the NT, for earliest believers, "God" was this one true God, to whose previous revelations the Jewish scriptural texts that came to be the Christian OT bear witness, and who believers insisted had given the surpassing self-revelation in Jesus. Hebrews 1:1-2 illustrates this view handily: "In many and various ways God spoke in former times to our ancestors by the prophets; but in these last days has spoken to us by a Son, whom he appointed as heir of all things, through whom also he created the world." From the earliest to the latest NT writings, no matter who the author, "God" is either explicitly or implicitly the one creator of heaven and earth and the uniquely worthy deity of the OT, the "God of Abraham, Isaac and Jacob" (Mark 12:26-27), the God in whom Abraham trusted (Gal 3:6), the God who promised David a perpetual inheritance (Acts 2:30-31), who gave the Law through Moses and is now more fully revealed in Jesus (John 1:14-18). In effect, the OT gave earliest Christians a dossier on the deity whom they worshiped and in light of whom they saw all other things.

This persistent and determined identification of "God" as this particular deity is noteworthy. It is certainly not simply an unthinking matter, something passively inherited from ancient Judaism as a historical accident and not really examined. Instead, this identification of "God" is

31

clearly deliberate, essential, and programmatic in the NT. Those earliest Christians whose faith the NT reflects understood "God" emphatically in this way, and this decisively shaped their whole understanding of everything else. As we shall see more fully later in this discussion, they certainly understood Jesus with reference to the OT God, e.g., as the fulfillment of specific divine promises and as the rightful messianic figure in whom "God" has now launched eschatological redemption. Likewise, they understood themselves with specific reference to this deity, as those who recognized and trusted obediently in the "God" who in Jesus had broadened the scope of the elect to include all those in any nation who turned to him, the former dividing wall between Jews and Gentiles now broken down in Jesus (Eph 2:11-22).

It is also clear that the ethics urged in the NT either directly invoke or presuppose the God of the OT. The Gospels picture Jesus' response to the question of what is the chief commandment as a direct citation of the OT exhortation to "love the Lord your God with all your heart, and with all your soul, and with all your mind, and with all your strength" (Mark 12:28-30 NRSV, citing Deut 6:4). In other texts, the centrality of the role of the OT deity as creator also, for example, provides the basis for handling various behavioral issues in the NT, including questions about foods (1 Cor 10:25-26) and the legitimacy of marriage for believers (1 Tim 4:1-5).

Yet it is clear as well that such a commitment to the God of the OT was neither inevitable nor universally embraced among early Christians. By the early second century C.E., Marcion presented the clearest proof of this.[11] Marcion insisted that there was an irreconcilable incompatibility between the deity presented in the OT and the true God now revealed in Jesus and the gospel. Whereas the OT deity was the lawgiver, through Jesus came a new river of grace and mercy. Whereas the physical creation came from the OT deity, the God revealed in Jesus called us to a spiritual and heavenly realm. Indeed, Marcion proclaimed firmly that the God revealed by Jesus was the previously unknown and true God and that the OT deity was shown as a pale and inferior being unworthy of worship.

Moreover, Marcion was not alone or the most severe in such views, only the most successful in commending his view of "God" to fellow Christians. There were still sharper distinctions between the OT deity and the true God in some of the so-called gnostic texts. In these, the OT deity is ridiculed and treated as a demonic imposter who sought to deceive people into thinking of him as the only deity. The statement from Isaiah 43:10-11,

> Before me no god was formed,
>> nor shall there be any after me.
> I, I am the LORD,
>> and besides me there is no savior. (NRSV)

is cited in several instances as clear proof of his insolent hubris.[12] The OT deity was the "demiurge" (*dēmiourgos*, "worker" or "craftsman"), whose act of creating the world of sense and matter was intended simply to provide himself with a sphere in which he could rule and a domain in which he could hold captive the souls of the children of light.[13]

Granted, the more severely negative views of the OT deity advanced among gnostic Christians seem never to have been widely successful beyond the (self-regarding) circles from which these texts originated. But, though we refer to them as "gnostics," in historical terms they were gnostic *Christians*, i.e., offering a radically different and competing version of Christianity. Moreover, Marcion's less severe contrast between the true God and the OT deity was certainly successful enough that more than sixty years after Marcion made his polarizing message known Tertullian thought it justifiable to compose an extended refutation of him.[14]

This provides further warrant for the observation that the unhesitating identification of "God" as the OT deity in the NT is noteworthy. Indeed, this emphasis on the OT deity as the true God may well be one of the factors that provided the perceived coherence of the emerging collection of writings that became the NT. It is certainly the case that in the second century (when these writings were circulating and acquiring more widely a use as Scripture in Christian circles) the major theological issue was the identity and nature of the Christian God. Christians of the time such as Justin Martyr (executed ca. 165 C.E.) asserted a strongly monotheistic view over against the dominant polytheistic culture of the time and equally strongly insisted that the one true God was to be understood as the OT deity.[15]

It is also important to note that "God" in the NT both is the one transcendent creator and ruler of all things to whom alone all nations owe worship and also is identified in very particular terms and can be addressed directly in prayer. The idea of one universal deity behind and beyond all particular deities of the Roman era enjoyed some favor among philosophical circles, but this ultimate/universal deity was typically portrayed as beyond any immediate contact and as so unfathomable in nature that one could really do little more than posit the deity's reality. The NT God, however (the deity also affirmed by subsequent figures such as Justin), combines a lofty transcendence and universal scope with an indelible particularity. As an example, note 1 Timothy 6:13-19, which combines references to "God" as the life giver on whom believers can safely set their hopes (vv. 13, 17) with descriptions of this deity as "he alone who has immortality and dwells in unapproachable light, whom no one has ever seen or can see" (v. 16 NRSV). Moreover, as we have noted, the one true God of the NT is also the deity witnessed to in the OT, who summoned Abraham from his pagan past and gave firm promises to him, led Israel out of Egypt, gave the Torah through Moses, and sent forth the prophets who spoke the "word of the Lord."

For Marcion, ancient gnostic Christians, and some other Christians through subsequent centuries, this particular association of the NT God with the OT was embarrassing, and this remains the case for some Christians today. But "God" in the NT is undeniably quite a specific deity, whose record of revelatory and salvific actions is known in the OT and in the gospel message and who is historically connected to very specific times, places, and people.

This particularity entailed also some polarizing consequences beyond the critical stance against polytheism already noted. The claims that the OT God had now sent forth Jesus as the self-revelation that surpassed all previous ones (including specifically the Torah), that this God thereby had widened the circle of the elect to include all nations, and that a right relationship with this God and a full participation in the elect now rested upon how one responded to Jesus, these all amounted to significant differences with the Jewish religious tradition. In effect, these strong claims challenged some central convictions and claims of ancient Judaism. In fact, we could say that the tension that erupted between the earliest Christians and some in their Jewish tradition was, from a certain perspective, fundamentally over conflicting claims about the same God. Early Christians (initially Jewish believers and then increasingly Gentile converts) claimed that the OT God was now to be identified with reference to Jesus and approached through him. Either implicitly or explicitly, this meant the relativization of all previous portrayals of and claims about this God, generating unavoidable (and understandable) tensions between the young Christian movement and the larger Jewish religious tradition.

It is an intriguing possibility that Jewish religious authorities of the second century and thereafter might have regarded Marcionite Christianity more favorably than the "proto-orthodox" versions. Marcion's firm distinction between the deity with whom Jesus was connected and the OT deity, Marcion's refusal to treat the OT as Christian Scripture, and his insistence that properly understood Christianity represented a totally new revelation, all these things might have seemed to Jewish leaders easier to accommodate. The more familiar Christian claims that the OT is Christian Scripture, that Jesus was sent forth by the OT deity, and that Christians are spiritual heirs with OT saints all effectively made for uncomfortable disputes with Jewish tradition. But Marcionite Christianity could be treated as a totally new and separate religion, which Jews could ignore. Marcionites and Jews had nothing to argue about, indeed little of anything to say to each other.

THE GOD WHO ACTS

I reiterate that the particular identity of the God of the NT is drawn entirely from the specific actions of this deity as witnessed in the OT and in the gospel. That is, in common with the religious outlook found also in the OT, the NT writings reflect the view that "God" is known solely through this deity's acts and that a right understanding of who "God" is can only be based on these phenomena.[16] The God of the NT is not accessible primarily or more fully through speculative reason, contemplation of nature, feats of ascetical effort, or mystical prowess. For instance, Paul writes that, although the creation bears the marks of the power and divinity of "God," human perversity (which extends even to cognitive faculties) typically yields a distorted perception and response to these things (Rom 1:18-21). In short, humans readily see things to fear or adore in nature, but the typical result is idolatry rather than a correct recognition of the one true God.

The God of the NT is described almost entirely in terms of God's acts of creation, calling, sending forth prophets, rescuing and vindicating, giving commandments, judging and punishing, and most importantly God's acts in Jesus, sending him forth, handing him over to redemptive death, and raising him and exalting him to superlative glory. So theologizing about "God" in the NT is essentially making inferences based on God's acts. In the view of "God" taken in the NT (as in the OT), anything else borders on empty speculation, and is liable to be both futile and misleading.

Consequently, there is scarcely anything in the NT that amounts to metaphysics other than the conviction that "God" exceeds the powers of human reason. In fact, there is very little extended discussion of "God" at all. There is certainly no attempt in the NT to portray "God unto himself," or this deity's "inner life," so to speak, for the only trustworthy knowledge of "God" is to be derived entirely from this God's own overtures toward the creation. In a classic OT passage, Moses asks to see "God" but is refused any direct vision (Exod 33:12-23), and GJohn echoes this emphasis on the utter transcendence of "God," insisting that "No one has ever seen God" (John 1:18 NRSV). For Paul likewise, "God's" wisdom and ways are unfathomable (Rom 11:33-35), albeit now declared in the gospel.

So, the reason that there is so little extended space given to discussion of "God" in the NT is not that "God" is merely presupposed or taken for granted. The OT reflects a similar approach, with little of extended exposition on its God. I contend that the actual reason for this lack in both OT and NT is the profound conviction reflected across the biblical texts that "God" can be known and described only in direct reference to this God's acts. So, typically, the biblical mode of theological statements is recitation of these acts with some limited inferences drawn in their light.

To use a Latin expression, statements about "God" in the NT focus on what we might call *Deus pro nobis* ("God for us"), that is, what we can know of "God" from this God's actions toward us. Moreover, the actions of this God are not primarily the disclosure of information about "God" in the service of theological speculation or mystical contemplation. The theophanic passages of the Bible tend to be occasions where "God" acts on behalf of, or against, other figures, thereby revealing something of divine purposes, character, and power. The divine acts recited and emphasized in the NT have to do with creation of the world, the election of a human line through whom a nation and other nations thereafter are to be brought to the light of the knowledge of this God, and other acts of rescue, preservation, judgment, and salvation culminating in Jesus. That is, these are acts of "God" for our benefit, on behalf of people, or otherwise directed toward them (e.g., in judgment). They are not stunts intended primarily to stun or mystify or to provide provender for philosophical reflection but, instead, are acts with intentions directed toward the creatures of this God.

This is why the statements about "God" in the NT are so heavily about this God's purposes and relational and moral attributes. So, for example, the NT emphasizes this God's love (e.g., John 3:16; Rom 5:5; 2 Cor 13:13), faithfulness to promises (e.g., Rom 11:29), care for creatures generally (Matt 6:25-33), righteous ways and opposition to evil (1 Cor 6:9-10), generosity, mercy, and grace (e.g., Rom 11:30-32). These are all theological claims that arose as reflective responses to the acts of this God that exhibit these qualities and attributes. I underscore the point, however, that the God of the NT is not presented primarily as an *object* of intellectual reflection but instead is an acting *subject*, the knowledge of whom is gained by this deity acting toward people and establishing with them a *subject-subject* relationship. In keeping with this, the human knowledge of this God advocated in the NT is to be exhibited primarily by participating in this relationship and not simply by ritual performance.

This produces some striking differences with the larger Roman-era religious environment. To cite one often overlooked, it was in that setting a remarkable claim that "God" loves humans. Indeed, many sophisticated pagans of the day would have regarded any such idea as ridiculous. It was certainly not a feature typical of the religious outlook of the time. In recorded prayer texts from the Roman period, various deities are praised for their power, their ordering of the world, their answers to prayers, and other attributes.[17] Some philosophers did refer to human love for beauty, understood in ethical terms as identified with the "good," and so with "god"; but the idea that the gods could love humans (as distinguished from the tales of erotic love for humans by the Greek gods) was not common.[18] Yet any reader of the NT will note the ubiquity and frequency of assertions about the love of "God."[19]

GOD AND JESUS

In the next chapter I discuss more fully how Jesus functions in the religious beliefs and practices reflected in the NT and the effect of this on NT discourse about "God." My more limited focus here is on some selected aspects of "God" as defined in the NT in light of Jesus. I propose that the emphasis on God's acts as the basis of knowledge of God is why in the NT "God" is identified distinctively and so emphatically with reference to Jesus, for the NT presents Jesus as God's greatest act of redemption and revelation. Indeed, we may say that in the NT just as Jesus' status is expressed consistently with reference to the actions of "God" ("the Father"), so in turn the identity of "God" is expressed typically in connection with Jesus. For example, the NT presents Jesus as sent forth by "God" (e.g., Gal 4:4), commissioned and acclaimed by "God" (e.g., Mark 1:11), empowered by God's "Spirit" to work miracles (Acts 10:38), and focused on God's "kingdom" (e.g., Mark 1:15). Jesus' crucifixion is both his own selfless obedience to "God" (e.g., Phil 2:8; Mark 14:36) and also the result of God's choice to hand Jesus over to this fate (Rom 8:32), and it is "God" who makes Jesus' death redemptive (Rom 3:21-26). Most emphatically, Jesus' resurrection is presented as "God's" vindication and glorification of him (e.g., Acts 2:36), and Jesus' unique status as "Lord" and his universal rule is conferred by "God" (Phil 2:9-11; 1 Cor 15:20-28). Whether in the Gospels or other NT writings, the overarching emphasis is on "God's" purposes, all events, claims, and characters (including Jesus) receiving their evaluation and meaning in light of these divine purposes. NT christological statements inescapably constitute at the same time *theological* statements.

Corresponding to this consistent articulation of Jesus' significance with reference to "God," there is a profoundly amended portrayal of "God" in connection with Jesus. The most concisely explicit expression of this is the new designation of the "God of Abraham, Isaac and Jacob" in the Pauline formula, "the God and Father of our Lord Jesus Christ" (Rom 15:6; 2 Cor 1:3; 11:31; Eph 1:3). This emphasis on Jesus does not, however, mean erasing the recollection of God's prior acts of creation and revelation. In the NT, as we have noted already, "God" is the deity of the OT, and the stories of this deity's actions in the OT remain of great continuing significance in defining "God." But the new emphasis in the NT is that "God" has now done something in Jesus so important that it represents a surpassing further disclosure of divine purposes, both illuminating the eschatological future and also casting a powerful retroactive light on all "God's" prior actions witnessed to in the OT. Everything is given a new meaning in light of Jesus, and Jesus in turn is the superlative vehicle of divine purposes, the new defining divine action in the light of whom one now can and must understand adequately what "God" means.

THE FATHER

We see this in the NT emphasis on God as "Father" (*patēr*), perhaps the most characteristic designation of God in the NT.[20] To be sure, the term is applied to God in the OT, occasionally in relationship to Israel generally (Hos 11:1), and particularly with reference to the Davidic king (e.g., Ps 2:7; 89:26-27; 2 Sam 7:14). In some Jewish texts, God is also specifically "Father" to the righteous (e.g., Wis 2:16). Indeed, in traditional Jewish prayer, one of the ways God is addressed is as "Our Father."[21] The term "Father" and the basic metaphor for "God" are not new in the NT. But it is fair to say that in the NT we find a far greater emphasis on "God" as "Father" and that the epithet acquires new connotations through being connected with Jesus' status as "God's" unique "Son."

The Pauline formula mentioned a few paragraphs earlier, "the God and Father of our Lord Jesus Christ," readily reflects this christological connection. In the NT, it is first and foremost in relationship to Jesus that God is "Father." Certainly, some NT writings deploy references to God as "Father" much more frequently and programmatically than others. For example, God as "Father" is much more heavily thematized in GMatthew than in the other Synoptics, particularly in comparison with GMark.[22] GMatthew uses the term for "God" far more frequently (44 times) than the other Synoptics combined. In GMatthew, "God" is called "Father" only in Jesus' sayings, however, the majority of uses in passages where Jesus gives directions and assurances about duties and expectations of disciples (17 instances in the Sermon on the Mount alone). These passages often reflect the use of "Father" in GMatthew to represent "God's" relationship to Jesus' followers as well. So, e.g., believers are instructed to pray invoking "Our Father in heaven" (Matt 6:9), and they are to live in the knowledge that "your Father" sees all and will act accordingly (Matt 6:1-18). It is noteworthy that in some sayings shared with GMark GMatthew replaces the word *theos* with *patēr* (e.g., Matt 12:50/Mark 3:35; Matt 26:29/Mark 14:25). Likewise, in sayings shared uniquely with GLuke ("Q" material), GMatthew exhibits a particular fondness for "Father" over other ways of referring to "God" (e.g., Matt 5:45/Luke 6:35; Matt 6:26/Luke 12:24; Matt 10:29-32/Luke 12:6-8).

But references to "God" as "the Father" (i.e., with the definite article) are particularly characteristic of GJohn. The term "Father" is used as a title for "God" 109 times in GJohn, more than twice as many times as in any of the other gospels. It is sometimes difficult to be sure whether statements are presented as spoken by Jesus or someone else or are comments by the Evangelist (e.g., John 3:35). But in the great majority of cases, it is in sayings of Jesus that "God" is referred to as "the Father" (e.g., 4:21-23). These are often in scenes of controversy between Jesus and Jewish groups or crowds, e.g., the numerous uses in 5:19-45 and 6:27-65. In some passages in GJohn the specific issue is Jesus' reference to "God" as his own "Father," especially 5:18, where the Jewish opponents take great offense at this, accusing him of making himself equal with "God," and also 8:18-20 (cf. also 6:32, 40). GJohn presents "God" as "Father" to Jesus in a unique sense and repeatedly refers to Jesus as "the Son" (e.g., 5:19-24), the definite article implying some sort of exclusivity in Jesus' filial status.

This idea that Jesus is in some unique sense *the Son* (of God) is by no means peculiar to GJohn. For instance, Paul reflects a similar view. Paul's references to Jesus as the "Son" (of "God") are not many, but every one of them implies that Jesus' divine sonship is unique. In each instance where Paul refers to Jesus as the divine "Son," he uses the Greek definite article (e.g., Rom 1:3; 8:29, 32; 1 Cor 15:28; Gal 4:4-6; 1 Thess 1:10). So, for Paul as for GJohn, Jesus is *the* Son, and "God" is "Father" to Jesus in a unique sense.[23]

Yet, as in GMatthew, so also more broadly in the NT, this emphasis on "God" as "Father" to Jesus functions as a basis for believers also to enter into a filial relationship with "God" and so to appeal to "God" as their "Father" as well. In the opening statements of GJohn we are told that to all those who received Jesus and believed in him "he gave power to become children of God," children "born . . . of God" (John 1:12-13 NRSV). In the distinctive Johannine *paraclete* material (John 14–16), Jesus encourages his followers to pray to "the Father" in his name and with confidence (16:23-24), and in the Johannine resurrection narrative the risen Jesus instructs Mary Magdalene to tell his disciples that he is ascending "to my Father and your Father, to my God and your God" (John 20:17 NRSV). Similarly, Paul refers to "God's" Spirit as conveying divine sonship to believers (Gal 4:4-6; Rom 8:14-17), a status that is theirs through Jesus' unique sonship. Indeed, in one passage Paul portrays "God's" redemptive purpose as the conforming of the elect to "the image of his Son, in order that he [Jesus] might be the first-born [*prōtotokos*] among many brothers" (Rom 8:29).

So, although the NT firmly ascribes to Jesus a unique divine sonship, "God" pictured as "the Father" to Jesus in an exclusive sense, this does not exclude others from a filial status with this God. Instead, the emphasis on this God as "Father" to Jesus seems to have generated a very strong sense that through Jesus believers also can enjoy a filial relationship with "God." Jesus remains *the* Son, but believers become other sons, with all the ancient legal connotations of the full inheritance rights of sons.[24] Paul's references to believers addressing "God" as "Abba! Father!" (Gal 4:6-7; Rom 8:15-16) show that the idea of this God as "Father" was meaningful for early believers and that it quickly found regularized expression in their devotional practices. The instruction to address "God" as "Father" in both versions of the "Lord's Prayer" (Matt 6:9; Luke 11:2) further shows this.[25] This central place of "God" as "Father" in early Christian devotional language and practice is also reflected in the greetings and salutations in the Epistles of Paul and other NT authors, which are commonly seen by scholars as echoing liturgical formulae (e.g., 1 Thess 1:1-3; Phil 1:2; 1 Cor 1:3; 1 Pet 1:2-3; Jude 1).

In sum, the God of the NT is "Father" to and for believers, to whom they look for care and comfort and to whom they entrust themselves. This paternal metaphor, however, is not presented in the NT as promoting maleness or as deriving from or giving some transcendent basis for paternity or patriarchy. Sadly, patriarchal attitudes have been all too often a feature of Christian tradition, but NT references to "the Father" never function to give divine validity to or privilege these or other forms of maleness. Instead, in the NT, "God" is presented as "Father" of believers primarily and directly on account of Jesus. It is Jesus' relationship to "God" as his own "Father" that is the paradigm and basis for believers to speak of and approach "God" using this epithet. That is, for Christians to refer to their God as "Father" is to express their relationship with "God" as mediated through and patterned after Jesus, and it is to designate themselves as those who come specifically to "the God and Father of our Lord Jesus Christ." The NT does not present "God" as "Father" to believers through creation or in some universalizing sentimental sense. Instead, for Christians to address "God" as "Father" is to affirm that they know this God effectually through Jesus and affirm Jesus' relationship to this God as his "Father." In short, the Christian practice of addressing "God" as "Father" originates as a profoundly *christological* statement.

The Living/Life-giving God

We see a similar adaptation of a theme from the biblical/Jewish tradition in the NT emphasis on the *living* and *life-giving* God. The contrast reflected in the NT between "the true and living God" and "idols" (e.g., 1 Thess 1:9-10) is, as noted earlier, carried over from biblical material such as Isaiah 43:11-13; 46:3-7 and Jewish tradition as reflected in Wisdom of Solomon 13–14. Moreover, this living God is also supremely the one who created life and continues to give life. Probably at some point in the Persian or Hellenistic period, the hope that this God will raise the righteous dead to life took hold and became an important part of the faith of many devout Jews.[26] The statement in Daniel 12:1-4 (NRSV) that "many of those who sleep in the dust of the earth shall

awake, some to everlasting life, and some to shame and everlasting con-
tempt" is usually cited as the earliest clear expression of this hope in the
Bible.

However, the powerful conviction that "God" raised Jesus from death
and has given him heavenly glory, which is central in the NT, makes
"God" as life-giver an important emphasis in a new way. In Jesus' resurrection, "God" acted in an unparalleled manner, giving Jesus divine vindication of the greatest kind imaginable. For Jesus' resurrection is not
presented as a restoration to ordinary life but was seen as a catapulting of
Jesus into the glorious/glorified life of the world to come. Whereas the
rest of the righteous dead still await the promised resurrection, "God" has
singled out Jesus, bestowing on him, uniquely, resurrected existence and
making him thereby the exemplar of what believers can hope for and the
assurance that their hope in "God's" readiness and power to raise the
dead is not in vain (esp. 1 Cor 15:20-58; Heb 2:5-18; 1 John 3:1-3).
Resurrection, thus, is presented as the essential means by which "God"
will demonstrate faithfulness to believers, and their hoped-for salva-
tion/vindication is directly patterned after what "God" did in/for Jesus.

Moreover, in a number of NT texts, "God's" resurrection of Jesus functions as the model of and basis for a new divinely empowered existence in
this world. For example, in Romans 6 and 8, Paul presents Jesus' death as
able to have mortifying effects on the sinful tendencies of believers and
Jesus' resurrection as able to provide powerful new moral resources to live
changed lives that please "God." So, in 6:1-11, Paul tells believers that
their union with Christ in his death should mean the virtual destruction of
their sinful tendencies, and their union with Christ's resurrection should
result in "newness of life" and being "alive to God in Christ Jesus." In 8:11
(RSV), Paul declares, "If the Spirit of him who raised Jesus from the dead
dwells in you, he who raised Christ Jesus from the dead will give life to your
mortal bodies also through his Spirit which dwells in you." The immediate
context indicates that by this Paul means both a future resurrection of
believers and also a present moral life of believers that exhibits radical
transformation empowered by the Spirit of the life-giving God (8:1-13).

So, "God" in the NT is emphatically known as the deity who raised
Jesus from the dead and exalted him to glory, which justifies and even
demands now that Jesus be proclaimed as "Lord" (e.g., Phil 2:9-11). But
God's resurrection of Jesus also serves to signal incomparably this God's
great power and purpose, which are to eventuate in a personal/bodily glorification of believers that is patterned after that given to Jesus. Also this

resurrection-power is available now to transform believers into true children of "God" (e.g., Eph 1:15–2:10). In short, the conviction that God had raised Jesus seems to have generated remarkably quickly a rich body of theological thought in which God as life giver was central.

A "PROTO-TRINITARIAN" GOD?

Clearly, convictions about the central significance of Jesus shaped the views of "God" presented in the NT. Moreover, in a number of previous publications I have emphasized how important it is that these convictions about Jesus and "God" found expression in devotional practices, especially practices in the setting of corporate worship. In view of the programmatic way that Jesus figures in the devotional practices and religious beliefs reflected in the NT, I have referred to a "binitarian" devotional pattern, a "mutation" in the devotional pattern and beliefs dominant in the Jewish matrix of earliest Christianity.[27] I do not have the space here to elaborate on the matter, but I must underscore the importance of taking account of early Christian worship practice as highly significant evidence that the NT reflects major religious developments, including particularly developments in how "God" is understood.

Indeed, to reiterate a point made earlier, we can say that in the view attested in the NT, "God" is so closely linked with Jesus and Jesus so closely linked with "God" that one cannot adequately identify the one without reference to the other. Jesus is the one through whom "God's" eschatological redemption is now bestowed and is to be consummated. But this central significance of Jesus is also retrojected through time, especially to the origins of the world, with Jesus (the "Logos" and "Son") depicted as the agent through whom God created all things (1 Cor 8:6; Heb 1:2; John 1:1-3). So, practically all of God's previous actions and self-disclosures can be retroactively understood in light of Jesus. To cite one particularly striking example of this, note how in John 12:37-41, Isaiah's vision of "the Lord sitting upon a throne, high and lifted up" is taken to be a vision of Jesus.[28]

To cite one further illustrative text, in Philippians 2:9-11, Jesus' exaltation by "God" even involves him being given "the name that is above every name" (NRSV) and being designated as the one whom all of creation is to acclaim as "Lord." This can only mean that Jesus is pictured here as sharing in "God's" own name with all that this connotes in the biblical/Jewish tradition. The obvious adaptation of Isaiah 45:23 (one of the most emphatically monotheistic passages in the Bible) to describe this universal acclamation of Jesus is a remarkable indication of the belief that this acclamation is now the required way in which "God" is to be glorified by the creation.

That is, we have in the NT numerous expressions of what seems to be a rather profoundly new view of "God" in which Jesus is crucial and integral. Yet it also remains the case that typically NT authors can distinguish "God" and Jesus. Jesus never displaces "God" in the NT, and the two are never pictured as in tension or competition with each other. Moreover, although Jesus is ascribed or is integrally involved in a number of "God's" attributes and actions, from creation through eschatological redemption and judgment, this never means that "God" fades or is diminished. In the NT, Jesus does not overwrite "God," and each is defined in relation to the other. "God" sent Jesus, gave him over to death, raised him from death and gave him glory (1 Pet 1:21), and ordained that Jesus be reverenced (Phil 2:9-11; John 5:23). Jesus obeyed "God" and redeemed believers for "his God and Father" (Rev 1:5-6). He is the "one mediator between God and men" (1 Tim 2:5; also Heb 8:1, 6; 9:15; 12:24).

In the "binitarian devotional pattern" that I mentioned briefly earlier, two things stand out: on the one hand the unprecedented and programmatic place of Jesus and on the other hand his clear functional subordination to "God the Father." As I have repeatedly stated, it is not "ditheism," the worship of two gods, but a new kind of monotheistic devotional practice in which "God" is worshiped typically with reference to Jesus, and Jesus is reverenced in obedience to "God" and to the glory of this God.

In a later chapter I explore more adequately the additional evidence concerning how "God's" Spirit is treated in the NT, but a few comments are essential here. I shall confine these to positing quickly two main points. The first of these is that in the NT "God's" Spirit is much more prominently mentioned than in the OT or the texts of Second Temple Judaism.[29] One reason for this is that the NT reflects the experiences of early Christians who believed that they had been blessed with rich manifestations of "God's" Spirit, evidenced in such phenomena as prophesying, healings, and glossolalia, as well as in powerful moral regeneration and the promotion of new loving relationships, especially among fellow believers.[30] Earliest Christians believed that they were experiencing the fulfillment of biblical prophecies of an eschatological outpouring of

"God's" Spirit (e.g., Acts 2:14-33). So it is little wonder that in their religious discourse reference to the Spirit of "God" features prominently.

My second point is that in NT writings the Spirit is linked specifically with Jesus in a remarkable and unparalleled closeness.[31] In some passages, Paul speaks of "God's" Spirit as "the Spirit of [God's] Son" (Gal 4:4-6 NRSV) and "the Spirit of Christ" (Rom 8:9 NRSV). The angelic statement in Revelation 19:10 (NRSV), "the testimony of Jesus is the spirit of prophecy," is likely another reflection of this, for the spirit that prompts prophets is typically "God's" Spirit (e.g., Joel 2:28-29). Also, in the Paraclete material in GJohn the Spirit of "God" is particularly linked with Jesus. Sent by "God" in Jesus' name (14:26), the Spirit is Jesus' advocate who will urge belief in Jesus and convict unbelief (16:8-11) and will glorify Jesus to believers and unpack further the true meaning of Jesus (e.g., John 16:12-15).

All of this means that already in the NT, discourse about and devotion to "God" typically involve references to Jesus and (with some important differences) the divine Spirit. That is, the NT already reflects a certain "triadic" shape to the early Christian experience of "God" and to discourse about this God. In the next two chapters, we examine more extensively the place of Jesus and the Spirit in NT discourse about "God," and in the final chapter I return to this triadic shape of "God"-discourse in the NT. So I confine myself here to a few comments.

Certain passages reflect this triadic shape rather clearly, such as the oft-used grace benediction in 2 Corinthians 13:13, which refers to "the grace of our Lord Jesus Christ, the love of God, and the communion of the Holy Spirit" (NRSV). To be sure, it would be anachronistic to read back into any of these passages the developed theological categories of the doctrine of the Trinity, which required a few centuries of debate and intellectual exploration. I do suggest, however, that this debate and the fervent intellectual exploration only reflect the prolonged effort to come to terms adequately with a pattern of discourse and devotion that was already traditional by the date of our earliest NT writings. In particular, the question of how especially to accommodate Jesus in belief and practice as a second and distinguishable figure along with "God" seems to have emerged in the earliest moments of the Christian movement. As Christians continued to explore answers to this question through the first three centuries, some of the subsequently traditional categories of thought were developed, such as references to "God" in terms of three "persons" and sharing one "substance." In this process, the Christian idea of "God" was elaborated significantly further and took on more explicitly trinitarian categories.[32] But, arguably, in the NT we already have what became the seeds of and impetus for this process.

SUMMARY

The God of the NT is emphatically particular, distinguished from all the other plentiful deities of the Roman era. "God" in the NT is the God of Israel, whose previous revelations are witnessed to in the OT. Moreover, this specificity of identity is matched by an answering particularity in worship, which is to be restricted solely to this one God. In the NT, as in ancient Judaism, the distinctive "monotheistic" stance is most typically and clearly expressed in the exclusive pattern of worship practice.

Knowledge of this God, who is presented as genuinely transcendent, is possible only on the basis of "God's" self-revelation, and what can be known of this God is limited to what "God" has revealed. So in the NT, theology is not speculative reasoning and is not much indebted to philosophical currents of the Roman period. Instead, the core form of God-talk is recitation of "God's" revelatory acts and words, and theological reasoning is essentially to make inferences (and they are limited) based on these phenomena.

But the most distinctive feature of the references to "God" in the NT is the strong association with Jesus. The decisive new revelation of "God" is presented in the NT as constituted in Jesus, in light of whom all "God's" previous revelations find their ultimate purpose in anticipating, preparing for, and now giving way to Jesus. Indeed, Jesus is so central to the understanding of "God" in the NT that one cannot speak adequately of this God without explicit reference to Jesus. Likewise, one cannot adequately worship "God" without including Jesus explicitly as a divinely authorized recipient of worship.

This "binitarian" devotional pattern (involving two distinguishable but linked figures) is the earliest expression of and impetus for what became the distinctive view of "God" in Christian tradition. In fact, one could say that the Christian doctrine of the Trinity originated in and remained mainly driven and shaped primarily by the need to find a way to accommodate Jesus adequately in the understanding of and reverence for one "God." It may not be sufficiently recognized by historians of dogma or contemporary theologians that the Christian doctrine of the Trinity is essentially a christologically shaped statement of monotheism.

To be sure, the earliest Christian texts reflect a triadic experience of "God," comprising the sense of "God" ("the Father") as the source and ultimate destination of all things, Jesus as the essential and unique agent of divine purposes through whom creation is now to be seen and through whom also redemption is provided, and the Spirit as the impartation and gift of "God" that is at the same time also the advocate and medium through which believers receive a filial status that derives from Jesus' own unique divine sonship. So, if it is a bit anachronistic to speak of "trinitarian" theology in the NT, it is right to see the roots of this doctrinal development in this body of texts.

CHAPTER THREE

"GOD" AND JESUS IN THE NEW TESTAMENT

INTRODUCTION

The key distinguishing feature of the presentation of "God" in the NT is the link with Jesus. Indeed, this link is so emphatic and Jesus' place in the beliefs, claims, and devotional practices reflected in the NT so prominent that one might ask whether "God" is pushed into the background or perhaps so thoroughly redefined with reference to Jesus as to constitute virtually a new or different deity. These might seem to be extreme suggestions, for certainly the NT writings continue to speak of "God" as well as Jesus and in various ways typically articulate Jesus' significance with reference to "God." But, more precisely, what is the relationship of "God" and Jesus in the NT, and what is the effect of the undeniably central place given to Jesus upon the understanding of "God"? These are the questions that occupy us in the following pages.

In a book published in 1924 entitled *The God of the Early Christians*, the distinguished church historian A. C. McGiffert contended that for most early Christians Jesus effectively was their deity and replaced any previous sense of who "God" was.[1] McGiffert argued that in the NT writings, we see reflected various efforts to rebalance and correct the more popularly supported Jesus-as-God piety by presenting Jesus as linked to, distinguishable from, and functionally subordinate to "God" ("the Father"). Moreover, in McGiffert's view, the subsequent development of the doctrine of the Trinity was a further prolonged and elaborate effort to try to "domesticate" (so to speak) populist Christian Jesus-centered piety in emergent "orthodox" circles. McGiffert contended that this effort was mounted by church leaders who viewed the putatively more populist religiosity with concern. The stance they promoted especially in doctrine and liturgy involved an understanding of deity in which Jesus could be included but which also differentiated "God" (the Father) and Jesus and maintained a strong connection with "God" as defined in the OT.

McGiffert's book attracted some critical engagement at the time of its publication but seems thereafter to have sunk from scholarly attention, and his thesis appears not to have won assent.[2] Yet, even if his claim that the NT represents an effort to correct a more popular early "Jesus-only" piety and theology is judged unpersuasive (correctly, in my view), there is certainly other evidence that in some populist Christian piety of the ancient world Jesus was effectively the sole "God" to whom prayers and praise were offered. That is, as McGiffert insisted, for some early Christians there was no meaningful distinction in function, relationship, or essence between Jesus and "the Father."[3] In short, for Christians in these circles, Jesus effectively eclipsed "God." Put another way, Jesus simply became "God," not God-the-Son defined in relation to God-the-Father but to all intents and purposes simply "God." Indeed, this may also be true of a lot of populist and theologically untutored forms of Christian piety across the centuries down into our own time.[4]

We cannot discuss later forms of Christian piety here, however. Instead, taking up the matter from an earlier chapter, our aim here is to consider further what the NT writings advocate and reflect about "God" in relationship to Jesus, specifically how the NT emphasis on Jesus' significance may affect the view of "God" advanced in these writings.

THE PROMINENCE OF JESUS

At the risk of noting the obvious, let us begin by taking stock briefly of the prominent place of Jesus in the NT. Clearly, Jesus is foregrounded in a way that appears to overshadow everything and everyone else. It is not at all difficult to see why so many studies of NT beliefs have focused on Christology.

For example, an elementary content analysis of the NT will show that the dominant concern in this collection of writings was to assert Jesus' significance. We have four full-scale narratives of Jesus' ministry, the

Gospels, which together constitute almost half of the NT.[5] Their individual particularities notwithstanding, in each of these writings Jesus is indisputably the central character. His teachings are authoritative, and the question of his person the central issue over which people divide. Those linked with him become his disciples, called to follow him; and there is no question that any of them is his equal, counterpart, rival, or successor. He summons them and they respond to his call (e.g., Mark 1:16-20). He sends them out and they further his mission (e.g., Mark 3:13-19; Matt 10:1-42). Jesus corrects and rebukes them, and in any difference between Jesus and them, it is clear that Jesus is in the right (e.g., Mark 8:31-33; Matt 14:22-33).

Over against his followers are those who criticize and accuse him (e.g., Mark 2:1-12; 3:22), some of whom even take steps to have him seized and executed. Although his message is the kingdom of God (e.g., Mark 1:14-15), in fact he is the polarizing force in the light of which everyone else in these narratives is portrayed (e.g., John 10:19-21). There is no question in the Gospels but that those who criticize and oppose Jesus are seriously wrong and show, at the least, their obtuseness to the divine truth and, at worst, their wilful rejection of it. In short, the drama of the Gospels is entirely to do with what response people make to Jesus, either to reject him (e.g., as a false teacher, sorcerer, Sabbath-breaker) or to affirm him (e.g., as Messiah) and align themselves with him as his followers.

As further illustration of Jesus' prominence in the NT, note, e.g., the formula, "Jesus is Lord," which seems to be the earliest extant creedal formulation, reflected in Rom 10:9-10; 1 Cor 12:3; Phil 2:9-11 (in this last passage the slightly fuller form, "Jesus Christ is Lord"). In the NT snapshots of early Christian proclamation in Acts as well, claims about Jesus' significance (typically expressed by honorific titles) are central. As examples, note the statement of "Peter" in Acts 2:36, declaring that "God" has made Jesus "both Lord and Messiah/Christ," and the characterization of Paul's preaching in Damascus synagogues as focused on Jesus as Son of God (Acts 9:19-20). In Acts 8:35, the thrust of Philip's conversation with the Ethiopian eunuch is described simply as proclaiming Jesus. Another famous statement placed in the mouth of Peter (Acts 4:12) declares that Jesus is the sole agent of salvation and his name uniquely efficacious.

Moreover, Jesus is central in NT references to early Christian ritual/devotional practices. I return to this topic later in this chapter, but it is appropriate here to provide some illustrations to make the basic point. For example, the confessional formula "Jesus is Lord" (*Kyrios Iēsous*) is commonly understood by scholars as reflecting a devotional action, an acclamation of Jesus characteristically set in the corporate worship context. Note also the ritual use of Jesus' name in Christian baptism, the common initiation rite in early Christian circles (e.g., Acts 2:38). Paul's rhetorical question to the Corinthians, "Were you baptized in the name of Paul?" (1 Cor 1:13 NRSV) rather clearly alludes to the use of Jesus' name in this rite. His description of believers as "all of us who have been baptized into Christ Jesus" (Rom 6:3 NRSV) is most likely another reflection of how central Jesus was in the practice of baptism and the understanding of the rite specifically as the initiation into a group in which Jesus was central.

Likewise, Paul's reference to the Christian corporate meal as "the Lord's Supper" (*kyriakon deipnon*, 1 Cor 11:20) must reflect an understanding of it as particularly devoted to Jesus and as a ritual declaration of his redemptive death (1 Cor 11:23-26). Note also Paul's portrayal of this meal as a corporate participation (*koinōnia*) in Jesus' body and blood (1 Cor 10:15-16), which further testifies to the centrality of Jesus in this ritual event. Indeed, Jesus is so central in the corporate devotional practice reflected in Paul's letters that he can refer to believers simply as "all those who in every place call on the name of our Lord Jesus Christ" (1 Cor 1:2 NRSV).[6]

In previous publications I have drawn attention to a whole constellation of devotional actions reflected in the NT writings in which Jesus figures prominently, and I have contended that there are no precedents or genuine analogies for Jesus' place in early Christian devotional life in other religious circles in the Roman-era Jewish matrix of earliest Christianity.[7] The key devotional practices, which seem to be characteristic in Christian worship circles already by the date of Paul's Epistles, are these: (1) singing hymns about Jesus; (2) prayer "through" and "in the name" of Jesus, and even to Jesus; (3) "calling upon the name" of Jesus, apparently a ritual invocation of him; (4) the use of Jesus' name in baptism; (5) the corporate "confessing" of Jesus, typically as "Lord"; (6) the common meal as "the Lord's supper"; and (7) prophecy uttered as inspired by Jesus. This constellation of devotional actions is prime evidence of what I have termed a "binitarian devotional pattern" characteristic of earliest Christianity, in which Jesus features prominently and uniquely along with God as the cause, content, and even co-recipient of devotion, including corporate worship.

The NT also presents allegiance to Jesus as the key controversial factor that will generate harassment and persecution for believers. Jesus is pictured as warning his followers that they will be hated by all "because of my name" (Mark 13:13) and will suffer persecution "on my account" (Matt 5:11). First Peter 3:13-16 urges believers to be unafraid of suffering for their faith, to "reverence Christ as Lord" and be prepared to give a defense of this stance if called to account. Also, Revelation (in which the prospect of persecution looms large) repeatedly refers to believers as those who testify to and suffer for "the word of God and the testimony of Jesus" (Rev 1:2, 9; 6:9; 12:17; 19:10; 20:4).

I trust that it is not necessary to illustrate the point further here. It is undeniable that Jesus is central in the NT. Affirmations of his validity and unique significance are central in proclamation and declarations of belief and form the key issues between believers and those outside their circles. In the NT Jesus is the one by whom believers typically identify themselves, and in their collective devotional practices he is explicit and central in a way for which we have no comparison in religious groups of the time.

THE OVERARCHING PLACE OF "GOD"

Yet in all the various presentations of Jesus' significance, "God" holds the overarching and crucial place. "God" is certainly not thrust into the background or sidelined. Indeed, as I indicated in an earlier chapter, Jesus' significance is typically expressed with reference to "God," and all the christological titles and claims of the NT really boil down to the one claim that Jesus is truly the unique expression and agent of "God."

Even the boldest christological assertions typically define Jesus with reference to "God," either explicitly or implicitly. So, "God" explicitly features in christological expressions such as "Son of God," "Image [*eikōn*] of God," "Lamb of God," God's "Servant [*pais*]"; and in some other titles "God" is obviously implicit, e.g., (God's) "Messiah/Christ," (God's) "Word," and "the Son."[8]

In other christological claims as well, Jesus' significance is expressed in reference to "God." For example, Paul refers to "the glory of God in the face of Jesus Christ" (2 Cor 4:6 NRSV). Colossians 1:19-20 (NRSV) asserts that "all the fullness of God was pleased to dwell" in Jesus and through him God works to "reconcile to himself all things." In a cluster of christological claims in Hebrews 1:1-4, Jesus is presented as the surpassing eschatological revelation of "God," as constituted by "God" to be "heir of all things," as the agent through whom "God" made the world, as the reflection of "God's" glory and the direct imprint of "God's" own being (*hypostasis*), and as now enthroned with "God" ("the Majesty on high"). To cite one further important example, in a passage now widely thought to derive from an early Christian hymn, Paul refers to "God's" exaltation of Jesus to a unique status (given "the name above every name") that all creation will be required to acclaim ("Jesus Christ is Lord"), this acclamation in turn redounding to "the glory of God the Father" (Phil 2:9-11).

The christological passages and claims that I have cited are all among the most exalted that we find in the NT, and the point to underscore is that in all *these passages* Jesus' status/significance is defined with reference to "God." Even in the few cases in the NT where the term *theos* ("god") is applied to Jesus, the contexts make it clear that Jesus is linked with "God" uniquely, not that Jesus replaces "God."[9] To cite the most familiar example, the immediate context of the statement "and the Word was God" (*theos ēn ho logos*) in John 1:1 makes it clear that for this NT author "God" and the "Word" are both distinguishable and yet also closely (indeed, uniquely) associated. The "Word" here may perhaps be thought of as sharing in some unique manner what "God" means, so to speak, such that *theos* can be applied to the "Word." Likewise, the famous acclamation of Jesus by Thomas in John 20:28, "my Lord and my God," must be read in the larger context of GJohn, including the statement by the risen Jesus just a bit earlier in the narrative that he ascends to "my Father and your Father, to my God and your God" (20:17 NRSV).

In a few other NT passages as well, *theos* may be applied to Jesus, but this is not so certain. In Romans 9:5, it is difficult to say with complete confidence whether the blessing upon "God who is over all" is to be taken as referring to Jesus or is to be read as "God who is over all things (be) blessed for ever, amen," i.e., as a concluding praise of "God" as the origin of all the things listed in vv. 1-5. It is likewise difficult to know whether to read the final words of Titus 2:13 as referring to the glorious manifestation of one figure or two: "our great God and Savior, Jesus Christ" or "the great God, and our Savior, Jesus Christ." In any case, the larger context of each writing (e.g., Rom 1:7; 8:3; Titus 1:1, 4; 3:4-7) makes it clear that each author thinks of "God" and Jesus as both uniquely linked and also distinguishable.

Let us return to the Gospel of John, however, for surely most readers would judge the emphasis on Jesus' divine significance in this writing as unsurpassed in the NT.[10] Yet this concern in GJohn to assert Jesus' significance is matched by an emphasis on "God" ("the Father").[11] One key passage will serve to make this clear, John 17, which in any analysis of GJohn must be taken as of crucial importance. It is highly significant that this body of material is presented as Jesus' *prayer* addressed to the "Father" (17:1). Granted, the Jesus of this passage refers to his (pre-incarnate) sharing in divine glory (17:5, 24) and speaks of himself and the "Father" as co-inhering such that they are "one" (17:21). But the prayer form of John 17 makes it clear that Jesus and "God" are also distinguishable and that Jesus is subordinate and subservient to the purposes of "God." One of the repeated claims in the passage is that Jesus has been sent forth by "God" (17:8, 18, 21, 23, 25). Indeed, 17:3 defines eternal life concisely as knowing two figures: "the only true God, and Jesus Christ whom you have sent." Simply put, GJohn combines the most astonishing claims about Jesus with an emphatic subordination of him to "God." Moreover, these two emphases are not the product of clumsy editing or the remnants of conflicting traditions; these convictions form the cohesive religious stance of the author.[12]

Undeniably, christological claims are prominent in the religious discourse in the NT, but all the key claims about Jesus directly implicate "God." Though phrased in varying ways, the key questions are whether Jesus came from and speaks for "God," whether his miracles are expressions of "God's" power or are Satanic, whether Jesus' crucifixion makes him a failed impostor or whether "God" has wondrously validated him by raising him from death, whether it is now blasphemy or obedience to "God" to accede to Jesus' validity and authority, whether the gospel of "God's" Son is foolish delusion or truly conveys "the power of God for salvation" (Rom 1:16; 1 Cor 1:18-25).

Jesus' Actions

We also see the significance of "God" in the ways that Jesus' actions are portrayed. As we have noted, the claim that Jesus was sent forth by/from "God" is emphatic in GJohn. But the claim appears in Galatians 4:4-5 as well, in the statement that "when the fullness of time had come, God sent his Son . . . to redeem those who were under the law" (NRSV).

Paul, for whom Jesus' redemptive death was so important a theme, refers to "God's" direct involvement in this event. In Romans 3:21-26, Paul portrays Jesus' redemptive death as the crucial historic manifestation of "*God's*" righteousness (v. 21). In packed phrasing that astonishes in its unprecedented claims, Paul then states that "God" "put forth" (*proetheto*, v. 25) Jesus as the provision for sins (*hilastērion*), and the demonstration (*endeixin*) of "God's" righteousness (vv. 25-26), which is now available to all who trust in Jesus and the redemptive efficacy of his death (vv. 25-26). So, as Paul portrays matters here, although Jesus is the named specific focus of faith and the unique person in whom redemption is now made available, it is actually "God" who directed all the events in view, "God" whose righteousness is manifested powerfully in Jesus' death, and "God" whose redemptive purposes are made effectual through it.

In other passages as well, Paul more briefly asserts "God's" primacy in Jesus' redemptive death and, of course, in Jesus' resurrection. Romans 4:24-25 contains what is thought by many scholars to be an early confessional formula in which Jesus' death and resurrection are both ascribed to "God," who is the clearly implied subject of the two passive verbs here, "handed over" (*paredothē*) and "raised" (*ēgerthē*).[13] In another passage (in this case with a likely allusion to the offering of Isaac in Genesis 22) Paul refers to "God" as "he who did not withhold his own Son, but gave him up for all of us" (Rom 8:32 NRSV).[14] Note also Paul's declarations that "in Christ God was reconciling the world to himself," and that "for our sake [God] made [Jesus] to be sin . . . so that in him we might become the righteousness of God" (2 Cor 5:19-21 NRSV).

Of course, the NT does not make Jesus an unconscious or unwilling victim. In some texts, Jesus' death is referred to as his own loving sacrifice for others. There is Paul's statement of personal devotion to "the Son of God, who loved me and gave himself for me" (Gal 2:20 NRSV) and also Paul's reference to "the love of Christ" manifested in Jesus' dying for all so that they might in turn live for him (2 Cor 5:14-15). There is the well-known saying in Mark 10:45, "the Son of Man came . . . to give his life [as] a ransom for many" (NRSV). Also, in the familiar Johannine saying, "No one has greater love than this, to lay down one's life for one's friends" (John 15:13 NRSV), Jesus is pictured as facing his looming execution in loving purpose.

But in still other passages, Jesus' death is described as also his obedience and service to "God." In the Markan Gethsemane scene, Jesus famously prays, "Abba, Father . . . your will be done" (14:36), submitting himself to the coming ordeal. In some of the most studied sentences in the NT, Paul states that, having taken the form of a servant, Jesus became "obedient unto death, even death on a cross" (Phil 2:6-8). Jesus' obedience here is to be understood as offered to "God" and is answered in the passage by "God's" surpassing exaltation of Jesus (2:9-11).[15]

The NT presents Jesus' resurrection as certainly the crucial vindication of him and the powerful confirmation of his status and significance. But the dominant way that Jesus' resurrection is referred to in the NT is as the *act of "God."* In perhaps the earliest NT writing, Paul praises the Thessalonian believers for having turned away from their idols "to serve a living and true God, and to wait for his Son from heaven, whom he raised [*ēgeiren*] from the dead—Jesus, who rescues us from the wrath that is coming" (1 Thess 1:9-10 NRSV). So, the statement that "Jesus died and rose again" (*anestē*) really involves the conviction that *"God" raised Jesus* from death, and in like manner "will bring with him those who have died" (1 Thess 4:14 NRSV). In short, Jesus' resurrection is not really presented as an expression of Jesus' inherent power or divinity so much as the exercise of *"God's"* power on Jesus' behalf.[16]

The emphasis on Jesus' resurrection as the act of "God" is echoed also in the Acts narratives of early Christian proclamation. For example, after positing that David foresaw the resurrection of the Messiah (in Ps 16:8-11), Acts 2:32 portrays Peter as declaring "This Jesus God raised up, and of that all of us are witnesses" (NRSV). Also, in his speeches in the temple (Acts 3:26) and to the household of Cornelius (Acts 10:39-40), Peter repeats the claim that "God" raised Jesus, and the same claim is also ascribed to others in Acts, including Paul (e.g., 13:30).

In other passages, Jesus is described as empowered by "God," and hence enabled to perform the miracles recounted in the Gospel narratives: e.g., Acts 10:38, "God anointed Jesus of Nazareth with the Holy Spirit and with power" (NRSV). Of course, the Gospel scenes where the Spirit descends upon Jesus are likely to be taken as dramatizations of this divine empowering of Jesus (e.g., Mark 1:9-11; Matt 3:13-17). As further illustration of this point, both versions of Jesus' response to those who accused him of sorcery ascribe his exorcisms instead to "God," whether "God's" Spirit (Matt 12:28) or the more memorable expression, "the finger of God" (Luke 11:20).[17]

Jesus' Purposes

When the NT writings refer to Jesus' purposes, they often portray his actions as directed toward "God," toward the fulfilling of divine purposes and intended to place believers in a positive relationship with "God." It will perhaps make this point more readily by noting, again, examples of this particularly from NT writings that are commonly seen as advocating exalted views of Jesus' own significance.

In Hebrews, for instance, where Jesus is portrayed loftily as reflecting the glory of "God" and bearing the imprint of "God's" own being (*apaugasma tēs doxēs kai charaktēr tēs hypostasteōs autou*, Heb 1:3), there is also a repeated stress on Jesus as priest and sacrifice to "God." So, e.g., we read that "God" directed and prepared Jesus through his sufferings so that he might be the more faithful and efficacious "high priest in the service of God" (Heb 2:10-18) and that Jesus "learned obedience [to God] through his sufferings" so that he could be perfected as "the source of eternal salvation" (5:8-10). As this high priest, Jesus was "faithful to him who appointed him [God]" (3:1-2) and so is able to sympathize with the weaknesses of believers (4:14-16). Jesus' eternal priesthood means that for "those who approach God through him . . . he always lives to make intercession for them" (7:25 NRSV). In another passage, Hebrews presents Jesus' death as his own priestly action, "through the eternal Spirit [he] offered himself without blemish to God" (9:14 NRSV).

Likewise, in Revelation, where the risen Jesus receives heavenly worship with "God" (5:9-14), the author also portrays Jesus as the one "who loves us and has freed us from our sins by his blood, and made us to be a kingdom, priests serving his God and Father" (1:5-6 NRSV). Moreover, in the song of heavenly praise in 5:9-10, the same note is struck, Jesus ("the Lamb") hymned as having ransomed all peoples *for* "God" and having made them "a kingdom and priests to our God."

For his part, Paul, too, makes reference to Jesus' redemptive actions as directed toward "God." It is noteworthy that the representation of Jesus in Hebrews as priestly intercessor on behalf of believers before "God" is anticipated by Paul in Romans 8:34, where he depicts the risen and exalted Jesus "who intercedes for us." From another angle, Paul also refers to Jesus as having willingly become "a servant to the circumcised" to show "God's" truthfulness, to confirm "God's" promises to the biblical patriarchs, and so that Gentiles too "might glorify God for his mercy" (Rom 15:8-9). That is, Paul here portrays Jesus' earthly mission as conducted totally in service to "God's" purposes. Likewise, in 1 Corinthians 15:24-28, Paul presents Jesus' royal status as conferred by "God," and also as intended ultimately to promote "God's" supremacy. Enthroned by "God" now, at the "end" when all has been subjected to him, Jesus will

hand over the kingdom to "God the Father" (1 Cor 15:24) and will subject himself also "to the one who put all things in subjection under him,
so that God may be all in all" (v. 28 NRSV).

If we return to the prayer ascribed to Jesus in John 17, Jesus' purpose is
depicted as serving "God," dominantly referred to in the prayer as
"Father." Jesus speaks here of having made the Father's name known and
having given the Father's words to those who were given to him by the
Father (vv. 6-8, 11, 26), and Jesus now entrusts believers to the Father for
safekeeping (vv. 9, 11, 15). In sayings familiar to readers of GJohn, Jesus
insists that he does nothing on his own but seeks only "the will of him
who sent me" (5:30), and does "the works that the Father has given" him
to perform (5:36).

Of course, the many Synoptic references to Jesus proclaiming "the
Kingdom of God" (e.g., Mark 1:14-15; 3:11) constitute yet another clear
way in which NT writings present Jesus' actions as intended to serve
"God" and to assert divine supremacy over all. In all the Gospels, Jesus is
undeniably the central figure, but he is consistently depicted with reference to "God" and as oriented toward divine purposes.

Devotional Pattern

I return now to another important (but typically overlooked) way in
which we can see the place of "God" in the NT: indications of devotional
practice. The NT writings are products of the intense religious life of
early Christian groups. These texts reflect and advocate beliefs and
behavior, but they also reflect something of the religious experiences of
early Christians and their patterns of prayer and worship. For them,
"God" was not simply an object of belief or a doctrine to which one gave
intellectual assent. Their lives were much to do with "God."

As we noted in a previous chapter, the Roman world was filled with
deities, and people generally affirmed the validity of them all. This means
that people generally were ready to join in the worship of any of the
deities as the opportunity arose and circumstances permitted. Residents
of any given city were expected to participate in the worship of the civic
deities, who were typically seen as protectors of the city. Likewise, when
one travelled to another city or land, it was perfectly acceptable, and
even expected, that one joined in the worship of local deities.

Early Christians, however, typically departed from these religious cus-
toms and defined "God" in a very exclusive manner in beliefs and also in

religious practice. For them, there was really only one true deity, at least only one deity worthy of worship, as Paul affirms in 1 Corinthians 8:4-6 (probably reflecting here the wording of the traditional Jewish confession of the one God, the *Shema*). Christians such as Paul certainly realized that there were many deities popularly touted ("there may be so-called gods," 1 Cor 8:5) and sometimes seem to have allowed that behind the pagan images were spiritual realities or evil forces that were not to be worshiped (e.g., Paul's statement that "what the pagans sacrifice they offer to demons and not to God," 1 Cor 10:20). But their belief in "God" meant that they could not in good conscience participate in the worship of the many deities promoted in their cultural setting.

In short, for early believers, "God" was a subject with profound behavioral and social consequences. Moreover, for them and in their setting it was worship that was the most sensitive issue and in worship where the line was drawn between what early Christians considered valid and invalid as "God." So, given the importance of worship practices for early Christians in defining themselves and their religious stance, it is appropriate to give attention to the indications of their practices in the NT writings as we seek to understand the place of Jesus and "God" in these texts.

We may begin by observing that prayers (especially, it seems, corporate or liturgical prayers) are typically described as directed to "God" ("the Father"). A selection of references will suffice to make the point. For example, in Paul's references to his own prayers and thanksgiving (typically for the recipients of his letters) he speaks of addressing himself to "God" (e.g., Rom 1:8; 1 Cor 1:4; Phil 1:3-5; 1 Thess 1:2-3). Note also Paul's prayer request to the Roman believers: "strive together with me in your prayers to God on my behalf" (Rom 15:30-31). The author of Hebrews exhorts believers to join in continually offering up "a sacrifice of praise to God" through Jesus (Heb 13:15-16). James 1:5-8 urges those who seek wisdom to petition "God." In John 14–16 there are several invitations for believers to address their prayer petitions to "the Father," although it is noteworthy also that in each case the petitions are to be offered "in my [Jesus'] name" (14:13-14; 15:16; 16:23, 26).[18] Acts 12:5 pictures the Jerusalem church as praying to "God" for the imprisoned Peter.

Beyond prayer, in references to worship more generally, "God" is typically the explicit recipient. For example, in Acts 24:14, the Christian Paul here portrays himself as worshiping "the God of our fathers," although it is significant that it is "according to the Way" (i.e., worship also shaped by the beliefs and practices of the Christian circles to which he attached himself). In his discussion of charismatic phenomena in the worship setting in 1 Corinthians 14, Paul speaks of prayers and worship as directed to "God." So, e.g., Paul pictures the outsider/unbeliever, seeing the operation of the Spirit in prophecy in the gathered church, as falling down to "worship God and declare that God is really among you" (vv. 24-25).

In two important scenes in Revelation where the seer, John, attempts innocently to worship the angel who reveals the apocalyptic scenes to him, the angel prevents this and directs John, "Worship God!" (19:10; 22:8-9).[19] Granted, as Richard Bauckham pointed out almost thirty years ago, it is also clear and remarkable that in Revelation Jesus is included as valid co-recipient of worship with "God." This is especially demonstrated in the scene of heavenly/ideal worship in 5:6-14, where an innumerable host sing praise to "the Lamb," followed by universal worship given "to him who sits on the throne [God] and to the Lamb."[20] But, as we noted briefly earlier, although included as co-recipient of worship in this text, Jesus does not displace or reduce the prominence of "God." Instead, Jesus is reverenced as the unique agent of "God's" redemptive purposes: "Worthy are you . . . for you were slain and by your blood ransomed people for God" (5:9). We see this inclusion of Jesus in worship to "God" also in Revelation 7:9-12, where again, an innumerable multitude stand "before the throne and before the Lamb" and sing praises to both (vv. 9-10). Yet the author then portrays these actions as all constituting the worship of "God" (vv. 11-12).

To underscore this point, I reiterate that, although Jesus is included uniquely in what we may call the "devotional pattern" reflected in NT writings, he is characteristically reverenced in connection with "God." Jesus is treated not as a second deity but as having a unique status with and from "God." This is unlike the pagan polytheistic pattern in which there are multiple deities, each with its own image, rites, sacred time, and often its own sacred space. Instead, in the early Christian circles reflected in the NT writings, the exclusivist worship of the one true God has this distinctive "binitarian" shape, Jesus featuring uniquely along with "God," yet with a pronounced concern to assert a monotheistic stance and avoid multiplying deities.[21]

As we observed earlier, however, Jesus clearly has a remarkable and distinctive place in early Christian devotion. We have already noted references to prayer as made "through" Jesus (e.g., Rom 1:8; 7:25; 16:27) or in Jesus' name (e.g., John 16:24). In other statements, praise and thanks are offered (to "God") "through" Jesus (e.g., Rom 7:25; 1 Pet 2:5), and "God" is glorified "through" Jesus (1 Pet 4:11). In all these references, prayers and praise are addressed to "God," but it is equally important to note the unprecedented role of Jesus. We simply have no analogy for prayers being offered "through" or "in the name" of some other figure, certainly not in Second Temple Jewish tradition. Moreover, to my knowledge, there is no parallel devotional practice in the wider pagan religious environment either.

In Paul's prayer wish in 1 Thessalonians 3:11-13, we have another indication of how closely Jesus was linked to "God" in his religious life:

> Now may our God and Father himself and our Lord Jesus direct our way to you; and may the Lord make you increase and abound in love to one another and to all . . . so that he may establish your hearts blameless in holiness before our God and Father, at the coming of our Lord Jesus with all his saints." (RSV modified)

"God" and Jesus are both implicitly addressed in the opening statement, and then Jesus specifically ("the Lord"), in what looks very much like a prayer. Note also the hope that the Thessalonians be found blameless "before God our Father" and that the crucial event in which their status will be examined will be the return (*parousia*) of "our Lord Jesus."

We even have some further indications of prayer appeals addressed directly to Jesus.[22] The dying Stephen is pictured as praying, "Lord Jesus, receive my spirit" (Acts 7:59) and asks that Jesus might forgive the crowd who stoned him (7:60). Although likely a dramatized scene, the author must have expected Christian readers to recognize Stephen's prayer to Jesus as a legitimate, perhaps even familiar, expression of piety. We have still more direct evidence of prayer to Jesus in 2 Corinthians 12:8-9, where Paul relates his repeated appeals to "the Lord" to be freed from the "thorn in the flesh" that troubled him. In the immediate context, and in light of Paul's wider use of the title "the Lord," it is clear that Jesus is the one to whom he made his appeals.[23]

Yet, in the NT writings, direct prayer to Jesus is less frequent than prayer addressed to "God." Moreover, in light of the larger context of the religious outlook reflected in NT writings, it is likely that prayers to Jesus were seen as implicitly authorized by "God's" glorification of him and that Jesus was seen as the unique agent and intermediary of "God" (e.g., 1 Tim 2:5).

There are still other indications of Jesus' close linkage with "God" in early Christian devotional life. This is likely reflected in the salutation characteristic in Paul's letters, "Grace to you and peace from God our Father and the Lord Jesus Christ" (e.g., Rom 1:7; 1 Cor 1:3; 2 Cor 1:2; Phil 1:2; Phlm 3). If, as is widely thought to be the case, the formulae in Paul's letter openings and closings were adapted from liturgical formulae, these salutations reflect a link of "God" and Jesus in the language and practice of early Christian worship. The grace-wish benedictions that typically appear in the closing lines of Paul's letters, likewise thought to derive from early Christian liturgical practice, are additional evidence of a remarkably prominent place of Jesus in early Christian devotion: "The grace of the/our Lord Jesus be with you" (e.g., Rom 16:20; 1 Cor 16:23; Gal 6:18; Phil 4:23; 1 Thess 5:28; Phlm 25).[24]

If we cast our attention beyond Paul's letters, we find still other striking indications of Jesus' link with "God." The epistle of James provides a good example of this. In the opening line, the writer portrays himself as "slave of God and the Lord Jesus Christ" (1:1), and elsewhere in this writing we see "God" and Jesus ascribed significant roles. Readers are told to appeal to "God" (1:5); and it is "God" who will confer the "crown of life" (1:12). The author urges "religion [*thrēskeia*] that is pure and undefiled before God, the Father" (1:27 NRSV), but he also exhorts his readers to "show no partiality as you hold the faith of our Lord Jesus Christ, the glorious Lord" (2:1). Later in the epistle, the author warns readers that "friendship with the world is enmity with God" (4:4 NRSV), and he urges them, "Draw near to God, and he will draw near to you" (4:8 NRSV). Yet, as is the case in other NT writings, the references here to the "coming [*parousia*] of the Lord" (5:7-8) and to the biblical prophets as having spoken "in the name of the Lord" (5:10) most likely point to Jesus.[25] Also, in 5:13-15, the anointing of the sick by church elders "in the name of the Lord" must reflect the use of Jesus' name in healing (and exorcism) referred to in other NT writings as well (e.g., Acts 3:6; 16:18), and so Jesus is "the Lord" who will heal in response to "the prayer of faith" and forgive any sins of the sick person (5:15).

Indeed, to repeat a point made previously, so prominent and characteristic is Jesus' place in early Christian devotion that Paul refers to fellow believers simply as "all those who in every place call on the name of our Lord Jesus Christ" (1 Cor 1:2 NRSV). The verb "call on/upon" [*epikalein*] in this statement seems to reflect its biblical use to designate prayer/worship of a deity (e.g., Gen 13:4; 26:25; 1 Kgs 18:24-26; Ps. 116:4). Also, we must probably take seriously Paul's statement here that this invocation of Jesus is the typical practice of believers "in every place." In confirmation of this, note that the practice is reflected also in Acts (2:21; 9:14, 21; 22:16). Moreover, the untranslated *"Maranatha"* expression in 1 Corinthians 16:22 probably derives from the worship practice of Aramaic-speaking believers, indicating that in these circles as well Jesus was addressed and invoked in the appeal, "Our Lord, come!" Indeed, as Moule stated, "a good case can be made for *Maranatha* as the earliest known invocation to Christ."[26]

It is important to observe that this remarkable devotion to Jesus is treated in the NT writings not as something optional but as *mandatory*, as obedience to "God." The devotional actions that we have surveyed did not emerge through some sort of liturgical experimentation intended to bring variety to devotional practice, nor were they the result of an unconscious seepage of pagan reverence for rulers and demigods or a deliberate deification of Jesus to make him "marketable" in the larger religious environment. Instead, from an incredibly early point, believers (initially circles of Jewish believers) felt themselves obliged to respond in these ways to "God's" will expressed in the glorification of Jesus. Likewise, it seems that in their eyes, to fail to reverence Jesus properly would be to disobey God. The most explicit statement of this is John 5:23: "The Father . . . has given all judgment to the Son, that all should reverence [*timōsi*] the Son just as they reverence the Father. Whoever does not reverence the Son does not reverence the Father who sent him" (NRSV modified). I contend that this Johannine text captures the sort of religious conviction that was rather commonly held in various early Christian circles. To illustrate this, I cite again Paul's statement of the divine intention that all creation should reverence Jesus as *Kyrios* (Phil 2:9-11) in response to "God's" superlative exaltation of Jesus.

In sum, the NT witnesses to a profound reshaping of previous Jewish devotional practice and discourse about "God" that seems to have been widely characteristic among earliest Christian circles. This constituted what may be termed a novel "binitarian devotional pattern," a distinctive "mutation" or "variant" form in Jewish monotheistic faith/practice of the time. Unquestionably, Jesus holds a prominent place in the devotional practices reflected in NT writings. Even so, however, "God" remains typically the ultimate recipient of worship, and the remarkable devotion to Jesus is intended as response to "God's" installation of Jesus as rightful recipient of this devotion.

CONSEQUENCES FOR "GOD"

In chapter 2, we noted some important features of how discourse about "God" is typically conducted in the NT with reference to Jesus, this especially evident in the ways that "God" is referred to as "Father" and as life-giver. In the final pages of this chapter, I want to explore a bit further what we may term the effects or "consequences" of the prominence of Jesus for the understanding and worship of "God" in the NT. In other words, how does the treatment of Jesus as in some unique sense divine affect how "God" is presented?

I commence by reiterating the point that in the NT Jesus' place in early Christian belief and devotional practices, though expressed in varying ways, is always presented with reference to "God." In short, all Christology in the NT is also, and profoundly, *theo*logy. All NT discourse about Jesus' high significance is at the same time discourse about "God," every particular christological title and claim also referring to "God" (whether explicitly or implicitly). Moreover, as we have noted in preceding pages, the devotional practices focused on Jesus are presented as also involving "God," whether as the authorization of these practices or as the one whose ultimate glory is served in them. That is, we may say that "God" is deeply implicated directly in all NT expressions of belief in and devotion to Jesus. Indeed, this linkage of "God" with Jesus is so characteristic and so profound that arguably it constitutes a significant adjustment in the understanding of the actions and purposes of "God" in comparison with the biblical (OT) tradition and the ancient Jewish religious matrix of early Christianity.

To cite an important example, in several NT texts the emphasis on "God" as the creator, which obviously is taken over from biblical tradition, is adjusted by the inclusion of Jesus as the agent of creation, the one through whom "God" created the whole cosmos (e.g., 1 Cor 8:4-6; John 1:1-3; Col 1:15-17; Heb 1:1-2). Granted, this probably draws upon Jewish traditions in which personified divine Wisdom or the divine Word is referred to in a similar role (e.g., Prov 8:22-31; Wis 7:22; 8:4; 9:1-4; Ps 33:6; and numerous references to the "Logos" in Philo of Alexandria).[27] In some texts this divine Wisdom is explicitly identified with the written Torah (Sir 24:1-23; Bar 3:9–4:4). So, the basic idea that "God" had involved a particular agent in creation was not entirely new.

Nevertheless, I contend that it is one thing to picture one of "God's" own attributes (whether in poetic or quasi-philosophical discourse) or

Torah as agent of creation and quite another thing to posit a real human figure of recent history as the one through whom the worlds were created. Despite the vividness of the portrayal in texts such as Proverbs 8 and Wisdom of Solomon 7–10, "Dame Wisdom" is not really a woman, and indeed it is most unlikely that these authors thought of Wisdom as really an entity separate from "God." The passages may play with and draw on ancient Near Eastern traditions of female consort-deities of male deities, but it would be a mistake to think that the authors uncritically imported this sort of idea into their religious outlook. It is much more likely that the personification of Wisdom served to make the point memorably that the one God ordered the world purposefully/wisely from its creation onward. Likewise, the linkage of Wisdom with Torah in Sirach 24 and Baruch 3–4 simply makes the claim that Torah is not an arbitrary or parochial set of rules but instead reflects this one God's greater purposes in creation. That is, Torah is to be received and observed as the written expression of God's intention for humankind, even "God's" larger purposes in the cosmos.[28]

As noted, NT writers seem to have drawn upon these traditions of divine Wisdom/Word/Torah as in some sense "God's" agent of creation. John 1:1-18, for example, is commonly thought to appropriate these motifs.[29] In other texts as well, such as Colossians 1:15-20 and Hebrews 1:1-3, it is clear that such biblical/Jewish traditions were appropriated to express key claims about Jesus.[30] But to ascribe to Jesus the role of "God's" unique agent in creation represents an unprecedented, even an audacious, move. No other human figure, not even Moses or any other biblical worthy is portrayed in this role. In first-century Jewish tradition, such figures as Moses enjoyed unquestioning esteem and were larger-than-life characters of a distant time (albeit of great continuing interest). Jesus, however, was a recent contemporary and also a controversial figure over whom opinions were sharply divided. In some texts, preexistence of some sort is attributed to biblical worthies, such as Moses (*Testament of Moses* 1:14), Enoch (*1 Enoch* 71:14-17), or Jacob (*Prayer of Joseph*), but none of these figures is said to have been God's agent in creation.[31]

Yet it is clear that NT texts do effectively posit Jesus as somehow the agent of creation. To be sure, in John 1:1-18, the author begins by referring to the *Logos* (Word), but there should be little doubt that this passage makes the most direct connection with the historical figure of Jesus. He is obviously the one referred to in 1:11-13, who suffered rejection and yet who also bestows a filial relationship with "God." Then, John 1:14

posits the *Logos* as having come in full fleshly/human mode, and just a few sentences later, in v. 17, we have the explicit naming of Jesus as superseding Moses and as being the one through whom "God's" grace and truth came. In the other key texts as well, such as Hebrews 1:1-3 and Colossians 1:15-17, it is clear that the human figure Jesus is ascribed the astonishing role of agent of creation.

Certainly, the texts in question also affirm Jesus' genuinely human origins and nature (e.g., Heb 2:5-18), and yet there should be no mistaking the equally strong and *direct* connection of the one who was born, circulated, and was crucified in Roman Judea and the "Word," "Image," "Son" through whom the worlds were made. To be sure, the NT presents him as "Jesus" only from his appearance in history, but the texts in view also seem to identify this "Jesus" rather directly with/as the agent of creation and in some cases (especially John 17:5, 24, but also 1 Cor 8:4-6) appear to ascribe some sort of real, personal preexistence to him.[32] That is, I contend that the NT writers in question affirm a rather *direct personal identity* of the human Jesus and the divine agent of creation. So, I do not think that we can take these texts as stating only in some looser way that in the figure of Jesus God's Wisdom and purposes were perceived by early Christians as supremely expressed in personal form. The force of the NT texts may well include the latter sort of claim, but their import cannot be reduced to it, even though some modern readers might find it a more congenial way to think of the matter.[33]

In other NT texts, Jesus is connected retrospectively with some of "God's" other prior actions and revelations witnessed in the Scriptures of Israel. Actually, in these texts the connection appears to be more alluded to than explicated, as if the authors expected their first readers to recognize the connections as already a familiar theme in their religious outlook. This seems to be the case, for example, in Paul's brief account of Israel's exodus from Egypt and wanderings in the wilderness in 1 Corinthians 10:1-13, where he makes the curious statement that the rock from which Israel was miraculously supplied drinking water was Christ (1 Cor 10:4; cf. Exod 17:1-7).[34] Paul here also appears to portray ancient Israel's disobedience in the wilderness as improperly testing "Christ" (or "the Lord," 1 Cor 10:9).[35]

There is another astonishing instance of this apparent retrojection of Jesus into the OT in John 12:37-41, where Isaiah's vision of "the Lord" exalted and enthroned (Isa 6:1-5) is declared to have been a vision of Jesus' glory. It is difficult to know whether we are to understand the

Johannine text as claiming that Isaiah foresaw the risen and glorified Jesus or had a vision of the postresurrection glory of the preincarnate Son (Jesus).[36] But, whichever one chooses, this Johannine text further reflects a striking retrospective understanding of the biblical tradition of the actions and revelations of "God" in which Jesus figures prominently.

In one of his numerous concisely expressed insights, Nils Dahl showed that the idea of Jesus' preexistence and agency in creation was likely a corollary of convictions about him as the Messiah whom God has now designated as the *Kyrios* through whom eschatological redemption is to be accomplished.[37] That is, in the logic of the sort of apocalyptic outlook of earliest Christian circles, Jesus' eschatological status/role signaled his "protological" significance/role as well. So, in the beliefs reflected in NT texts, although revealed "late in time" and designated "Lord" and divine "Son" in God's resurrection and exaltation of him (e.g., Rom 1:3-4; Phil 2:9-11; Heb 1:3; Rev 5:9-10), Jesus was in fact always the unique and divine agent of God's purposes from creation onward.

This sort of conviction is expressed in Colossians 1:11-20, for instance. Note how the author so easily links statements about Jesus as "[God's] beloved Son, in whom we have redemption" with references to Jesus as the one in whom and for whom all was created and in whom "all things hold together" (1:16-17), the one in whom "all the fullness of God was pleased to dwell" (1:19), and the one through whose bloody crucifixion "God" will "reconcile to himself all things" (1:20). Likewise, 1 Peter 1:18-21 seamlessly combines statements about the redemptive benefits of "the precious blood of Christ" (vv. 18-19) with claims that "he was destined before the foundation of the world, but was made manifest at the end of times for your sake" (v. 20).

I want to emphasize again that all these claims about Jesus are equally statements about "God," implicating "God" at every step, both in the present and its eschatological consummation and also retrospectively in the biblical (OT) record of divine revelation. Certainly, divine purposes are redefined to make emphatic Jesus' crucial place as the "beloved Son" through whom universal redemption is now proclaimed, as the one through whom worship is now to be given to "God," and as the one through whom these divine purposes are to be consummated. Of course, the ultimate result of all this is, to use the phrasing from Philippians 2:11, "the glory of God the Father" (and note Rom 11:36). Elsewhere Paul also states that the heavenly enthronement of Jesus involved in his resurrection is intended to secure the submission of everything to him and that this in turn is to eventuate in Jesus' self-subjection to "God the Father" (1 Cor 15:23-24) so that "God might be everything in everything" (v. 28). It requires little reflection, however, to realize that the glory of "God" and the triumph of "God's" purposes are so closely linked with Jesus as to make Jesus essential to them. That is, arguably, "God" is thereby redefined in a significant degree with reference to Jesus.

It is a related observation that the human elect who feature in the purposes of "God" are also redefined. The NT emphasis that Jesus is the one in whom eschatological redemption is provided involves the redefinition of the company of the redeemed with reference to him. So, e.g., we have the Gospel warning that one's response to Jesus ("the Son of Man") will have decisive consequences in the eschatological day of judgment (Mark 8:38; Matt 10:32-33; Luke 12:8-9). Acts declares that Jesus is the one in whose name salvation is now offered and that a positive response to the gospel is required of Jews (e.g., Acts 3:36-40; 4:8-12) and Gentiles alike (e.g., Acts 17:30-31). Although Paul insists that the Jewish people retain a special place in God's ultimate purposes (esp. Rom 11:25-32), he treats Jewish rejection of the gospel as misguided and disobedience to "God" (Rom 10:1-4, 18-21), and he insists that acclamation of Jesus as "Lord" is now the enlightened response to "God" (Rom 10:8-13). For Paul, the "Deliverer [who] will come from Zion" to "banish ungodliness from Jacob" is obviously Jesus, through whom "all Israel will be saved" (Rom 11:26). The "gospel of God" concerns this God's Son, "Jesus Christ our Lord" (Rom 1:1-4), and this gospel is "the power of God for salvation to everyone who believes [it]," whether Jew or Greek (Rom 1:16-17).

In some NT texts, we even have the idea that this Jesus-defined company of the redeemed were identified as such in divine purposes from the creation of the world. There is probably a brief reference to this idea in Paul's statement that "those whom [God] foreknew he also predestined to be conformed to the image of his Son," and those predestined by "God" are also then called through the preaching of the gospel, declared righteous in their believing response, and are to be "glorified" with a filial status patterned after Christ's (Rom 8:29-30, and vv. 19-23 NRSV). Ephesians 1:3-10 more explicitly portrays "God" as having chosen and destined the redeemed "in Christ" and "before the foundation of the world" as part of the divine purpose "which he set forth in Christ as a plan for the fullness of time, to unite all things in him." In a slightly more oblique statement, Revelation 17:8 contrasts those who worship "the beast" with those whose names have been written "in the book of life before the foundation of the world," and in 13:8 we have a similar state-ment that specifies these names as written "in the book of life of the Lamb."[38] As Dahl noted in the essay mentioned a few paragraphs earlier, in the NT this idea of the redeemed as somehow known and "chosen" from the creation of the world is directly based on the conviction that "God" destined Jesus as the chosen instrument of eschatological redemp-tion from "the foundation of the world." So, Jesus is the one who now defines the redeemed/elect, and the elect are such "in him."[39]

The undeniable point here is that in these statements "God's" elect are identified with reference to Jesus. It is obedience to the gospel and the acclamation of Jesus as Lord that now constitute the necessary human response to "God," and the company of "God's" elect are now all those, from Israel and also the Gentiles, who respond to this God through Jesus (e.g., Rom 4:13-17, 23-24; 8:12-13). Given that the "God" of the OT is so closely identified with reference to Israel in particular, and in Jewish tradition so much revealed in Torah, this redefining of the elect also has consequences for understanding who this God is. Here again, we see that the understanding of what "God" means is not simply taken over unal-tered and presupposed but undergoes a significant development in the NT.

Yet it is not a simple matter. As we noted clearly in chapter 2, in the NT "God" is not simply or entirely defined with reference to Jesus, for the OT testimony continues to be treated as valid. Indeed, Jesus is typi-cally defined with reference to the "God" revealed in the Scriptures of Israel. It is *this* God, and not some other or some generic deity, who sent forth Jesus in fulfillment of biblical prophecies and promises (e.g., Gal 4:4-6). Of course, the title "Christ" reflects the claim that Jesus is the eschatological figure in whom the prophetic purposes of this "God" are now focused. Certainly, some NT writings emphasize this OT connection more strongly than others, but it is there explicitly or implicitly in them all. Indeed, this is one of the key things that unites the NT as a collection.

So, however much the prominence of Jesus in the NT involves a sig-nificant modification in how "God" is understood, it would be an over-simplification to think of the NT as presenting a new deity. Granted, Marcion certainly did, and he seems to have enjoyed an impressive suc-cess among other Christians. But the NT "God" is not Marcion's, not a previously unknown deity, but the same God to whom the OT testifies, and who now in Jesus has brought decisively toward fulfillment purposes that were set from the beginning of creation (e.g., Heb 1:1-2).

So a developed understanding of "God" in the light of Jesus involves *both* a full continuity with the OT witnesses *and also* a significant further development. As noted earlier, in various publications over a number of years, I have referred to earliest Christian Jesus-devotion as involving a significant "mutation" in Jewish devotion to the one God.[40] Similarly, we could say that in the NT the prominence of Jesus and the specific ways in which Jesus is linked with divine purposes have major consequences for "God." The collective force of the NT on this point is that "God" must now be understood *and engaged devotionally* in light of Jesus. Insofar as Jesus (as described in the NT) manifests divine purposes, "God" is inseparably connected to Jesus, and theological reflection on "God" must now reflect the prominence and eschatological centrality of Jesus.

CHAPTER FOUR

THE SPIRIT AND "GOD" IN THE NEW TESTAMENT

THE SPIRIT AND "GOD"

W e have noted already that discourse about "God" in the NT has what we may call a "triadic shape" and that this helped substantially to generate and influence subsequent Christian doctrinal reflections that led to the developed doctrine of the Trinity. That is, the NT is replete with references to "God" ("the Father"), to Jesus as the unique expression of divine purposes who shares in the glory of "God," and also to the divine Spirit. Although the most distinctive feature of NT discourse about "God" is the significance ascribed to Jesus (as discussed in a previous chapter), the references to the divine Spirit certainly form another crucially important component. There is, however, neither space nor need here to attempt a full-scale study of the Spirit in the New Testament.[1] Instead, the more modest aims in this chapter are to note how references to the divine Spirit function in NT discourse about "God" and to assess the broad effects upon the representations of "God" in the NT.[2]

Perhaps the first and most ready observation to make is the sheer frequency and extent of references to the divine Spirit in NT writings.[3] Of the 379 uses of the word *pneuma* (in its various forms) in the Greek NT, in approximately 275 instances the reference is to the divine Spirit, the remaining instances split among various referents, including human (approx. 47 instances, e.g., Matt 26:41; 27:50) and demonic spirits (approx. 38 instances, e.g., Matt 8:16; 10:1; 12:43, 45). Obviously, the divine Spirit is by far the largest single referent in the NT uses of *pneuma*. Moreover, the divine Spirit is referred to in every NT writing except for the two small texts 2 John and 3 John. So, both in frequency and distribution, we are considering a major component in NT discourse about "God," references to the Spirit forming part of this discourse reflected broadly across the NT. That is, to judge from the writings that make up the NT (and which are commonly thought to derive from various early Christian settings and circles), the Spirit was an important feature of the religious discourse of a wide swath of first-century Christians.

BIBLICAL/JEWISH BACKGROUND

Of course, however, references to the (divine) "Spirit" did not commence with early Christians. The dominant background influence on their use of this term was the biblical/Jewish tradition, where the Spirit was already part of discourse about "God." In the Hebrew Bible (OT), there are copious references (approx. 75) to the divine Spirit, from the creation account (Gen 1:2) onward at various points.[4] The frequent phrasings are "the/my Spirit" (Hebrew: [*ha*] *ruach*, approx. 29 instances, e.g., Gen 6:3; Num 11:26; approx. 10 in Ezekiel, e.g., Ezek 3:12), "the Spirit of the LORD" (Hebrew: *ruach Yahweh*, approx. 25 instances, e.g., Judg 3:10; 1 Sam 10:6; Isa 11:2), "the Spirit of God" (*ruach Elohim*; 11 instances, e.g., Gen 41:38; Exod 31:3; 35:31; and one instance of *ruach El* in Job 33:4). "Holy Spirit" occurs only rarely, however ("his Holy Spirit," *ruach qadsho*, Isa 63:10-11; "your Holy Spirit," *ruach qadshᵉkha*, Ps 51:13), which makes an interesting contrast with the NT, as we shall see.[5] In the Greek OT (LXX), the word *pneuma* typically renders *ruach* when used for the divine Spirit and for the human spirit too.

In the OT the divine Spirit is typically manifested as a special power from "God" given to individuals to enable them for particular tasks or roles. Although expressed through human personalities, the Spirit typically "comes from God in special situations and under special circumstances," and is an entity distinguishable from the human person.[6] For instance, Moses refers to Bezalel as filled with divine Spirit, enabling him to lead in the artisan work devoted to fashioning the tabernacle (Exod 35:30-35). In other texts, the divine Spirit enables humans to prophesy: e.g., the elders of Israel (Num 11:25-29), Balaam (Num 24:2), Saul (1 Sam 10:6-10; 11:6), and Micah (3:8). In the book of Judges, the divine

Spirit frequently emboldens individuals to take decisive action on behalf of oppressed Israelite tribes (e.g., Othniel, 3:10; Gideon, 6:34; Jephthah, 11:29), and in several references empowers Samson's mighty feats (14:6, 19; 15:14). In all these cases, we have particular individuals gifted with the Spirit for specific tasks.

It is also worth noting, however, that some OT texts look forward to a time of future divine blessings, prominent among which is the prospect of a richer bestowal and activity of the Spirit. For instance, there is the prophetic promise that the divine Spirit will be rather fully active in the scion of the restored Davidic royal line (Isa 11:1-3), in the "servant" in whom God delights (Isa 42:1), and even among the descendents of Israel more broadly (Isa 44:3). This idea of a wider sharing of the experience of the Spirit is also famously projected in Joel 2:28-29 (MT and LXX 3:1-5, a text explicitly cited in Acts 2:16-21 as fulfilled in the phenomena of the Pentecost episode). In a lengthy oracle, there is the following divine promise:

> I will pour out my spirit on all flesh;
>   your sons and your daughters shall prophesy,
> your old men shall dream dreams,
>   and your young men shall see visions.
> Even on the male and female slaves,
>   in those days, I will pour out my spirit." (Joel 2:28-29 NRSV)[7]

When we consider the extracanonical texts of ancient Jewish tradition, the divine Spirit is most often associated with prophecy.[8] This is the case in texts from a Palestinian provenance (e.g., *Jub.* 25:14; 31:12; *1 En.* 91:1; 1QS 8:15-16) and those that reflect a more overtly Hellenized influence (Philo, but also Josephus). In his extensive analysis of references to the divine Spirit in selected Jewish texts, Levison concluded, "Among the effects of the [divine] spirit prophecy is most pervasive," noting that Philo, Josephus, and Pseudo-Philo even occasionally add references to the divine Spirit in discussions of OT prophets/prophecy, and that these writers "are themselves part of the creative process which develops and deepens the association of the spirit and prophecy."[9] Levison pointed out, however, that in ancient Jewish texts the divine Spirit is also associated with creation of the world, sanctification of the righteous, eschatological blessings, and human enablement.[10] In his survey of a wide range of ancient Jewish texts, Menzies judged that there is a dominant association of experience of the Spirit with prophetic inspiration, special insight, and knowledge (granted to the pious or prophet or Messiah).[11]

A number of these references to the Spirit look back to OT prophets, although some also hold out the continuing prospect of special religious insight conferred on devout individuals by the Spirit. In the Qumran texts, however, and especially in the "Hymns" collection (*Hodayot*), the Spirit is portrayed as "the dynamic of the religious life of the community."[12] Although in some texts "God" is said to have placed within humans at their birth two spirits, a spirit of truth and a spirit of deceit (the most frequently cited instance is a passage in "The Rule of the Community," 1QS 3:17-19), the far more dominant emphasis is on the divine Spirit as an external power that assists the righteous to please "God" (e.g., 1QS 3:6-11; 4:20-23). From his detailed analysis of the use of the Hebrew word *ruach* in the Qumran nonbiblical texts, Sekki concluded that they reflect an understanding of the divine Spirit as "an eschatological gift of God's power," which members of the Qumran community could hope for and even experience in their religious life.[13] To get a small taste of these references to the Spirit, we may note 1QH 15:6-7.

> I give you thanks, Lord,
> because you have sustained me with your strength,
> you have spread your holy spirit [*ruach qodesh^ekha*] over me so that I will not stumble,
> you have fortified me against the wars of wickedness,
> and in all their calamities you have not discouraged (me) from your covenant.[14]

The Qumran texts are also of interest in reflecting a preference for the expressions "Holy Spirit" and "Spirit of Holiness" (Sekki counted nineteen instances of the relevant Hebrew constructions in all, including eleven instances in the *Hodayot*). As noted already, "Holy Spirit" is not frequent in the OT (even allowing for the few additional uses in the Greek versions of Daniel and in Wisdom of Solomon); but this is the clearly favored way of referring to the Spirit in the NT (approx. 90 instances). Similarly, in both the Qumran texts and the NT writings the next most frequently used expression is simply "(the) Spirit" (without other modifying terms), seven instances in the Qumran texts and 64 instances in the NT.

But, although the OT is clearly the key influence on the NT references to the divine Spirit, and ancient Jewish extracanonical texts show that the Spirit was a feature of religious discourse in the Jewish tradition in which the first Christian circles emerged, it is rather clear that the NT treatment of the Spirit is distinctive in a number of ways. I underscore the ready observation that there is simply a far greater place of the Spirit in the religious discourse in the NT texts, obviously reflected in the far greater frequency of references to the Spirit. Compare the approximately 75 references to the divine Spirit in the Hebrew OT with the 275 references in the NT. When we take account of the far larger size of the OT (whether the Hebrew or Greek OT), the comparison is even more striking.[15] Likewise, although the divine Spirit figures somewhat in the religious discourse of a number of ancient Jewish extracanonical texts, the enormously greater frequency of references to the Spirit in the NT is obvious and highly significant. Even the relatively frequent references to the Spirit in the Qumran texts (compared with other extracanonical Jewish writings) are dwarfed by the far greater number in the NT. Compare, for example, the 27 references to the Spirit in Paul's Epistle to the Romans alone, or the 58 references in Acts, with the total of 35 references to the Spirit identified by Sekki in the whole corpus of nonbiblical Hebrew texts from Qumran.[16]

The most reasonable inference is that this far greater frequency and prominence of references to the Spirit in the NT likely reflects the religious life and discourse of early Christian circles generally. It is commonly accepted that the quantity of references to the Spirit in the Qumran texts reflects an intense piety and likely the cultivation of religious experiences in which divine blessings of the last days were believed to be already bestowed (corporate worship being a prime setting for such experiences).[17] The far greater number of references to the Spirit in the NT, thus, probably reflects a still more intense level of religious experience ascribed to the Spirit in early Christian groups. Certainly, the prominence of the Spirit in NT discourse is unmatched in either OT or extracanonical Jewish texts and is also not found in pagan religious discourse of the time.

THE PLACE OF THE SPIRIT IN THE NT

I turn now to add some further specifics about the many references to the Spirit in the NT, with a view to making some broad observations about how the Spirit functions in NT discourse about "God." Reflecting the influence of the OT particularly, NT references rather consistently represent the Spirit as a power that originates in "God" and is given to humans. That is, the divine Spirit is typically distinguished from the human spirit or soul. We see a ready example of this in Romans 1 where Paul first refers to "the Spirit of holiness" as involved in Jesus' resurrection (v. 4), and then to serving God "with my spirit [in] the gospel of his Son" (v. 9 NRSV). Granted, in some passages the referent is not immediately clear (e.g., in 1 Cor 5:3 does "*parōn de tō pneumati*" mean "present in [my] spirit," or "present in the [divine] Spirit"?).[18] But in most cases it is clear that the NT texts distinguish the divine Spirit from the human spirit. NT texts refer to the human spirit (*pneuma* used with this latter sense about forty times) as essentially a faculty or component of the human person, the inward and invisible aspect of individual life.[19] Indeed, in 1 Corinthians 2:10-13, Paul makes a direct comparison of how the divine Spirit "searches everything, even the depths of God" and how an individual's thoughts are really known only to that person's own spirit.

It is worth exploring further some NT designations of the divine Spirit, at this point particularly those that enable comparisons with uses in the OT and extracanonical Jewish texts. Later in this chapter, I turn to some other designations that are unique to the NT. As noted already, the predominant expression in the NT is "the Holy Spirit," the equivalent Hebrew expressions used seldom in the OT. The preference for "Holy Spirit" and/or "Spirit of holiness" in the Qumran texts mentioned earlier, however, is interesting, suggesting that in these texts and the NT we have (likely independent) witnesses to an emphasis in early Jewish tradition on the religious character of the divine Spirit as *holy*, underscoring a distinction from either human or malevolent spirits ("demons").

The next most frequently occurring expression is simply "The Spirit," without any modifier (e.g., nearly 50 instances in the Pauline corpus, approx. 8 times in John, and approx. 13 times in Revelation).[20] The equivalent phrase is likewise not frequent in the OT (Num 11:26; 27:18; and several in Ezekiel, e.g., 1:12; 3:12; 8:3) or in extracanonical texts, and Swete was probably correct to contend that this frequent use of "the Spirit" without further identification signals the very prominent place that the divine Spirit held in the religious life and discourse of the Christian circles reflected in the NT texts.[21] That is, the Spirit (of "God") was so familiar in their religious experience and discourse that "the Spirit" could serve adequately as a way of referring to it.

A major emphasis in the NT is that the Spirit is now freely given by "God" and so is powerfully and regularly operative in the lives of believers individually and collectively. There is a rich variety of verbs used to describe the divine action of giving the Spirit, of which the following are illustrative. In Acts 2:33, the exalted Jesus is portrayed as "having received from the Father the promise of the Holy Spirit," and then as having "poured out" the Spirit upon the gathered believers in the Pentecost scene, the verb "poured out" echoing the prophetic promise of a future rich dispensation of the Spirit (Joel 2:28; in MT 3:1). In other passages, Acts depicts believers as "filled" with the Spirit (e.g., 2:3; 4:31) or receiving the Spirit and the Spirit "falling upon" them (e.g., 8:14-17; 10:44-47). Paul refers to the Spirit as divinely given (e.g., 1 Thess 4:8) and sent forth (e.g., Gal 4:6) and memorably writes of God's love as "poured into our hearts through the Holy Spirit that has been given to us" (Rom 5:5 NRSV). Several NT passages vividly picture being "baptized" in/with the Spirit (Matt 3:11; Luke 3:16; Acts 1:5, the term depicting metaphorically a powerful immersion in the Spirit.

These and other references further reflect both the influence of OT language and also the intensity of focus on the Spirit in earliest Christian religious discourse. Indeed, we may say that in the NT generally the Spirit is the characteristic agency of divine power and presence, especially within and among believers. For example, Paul claims that the Spirit brings new inner/moral life-power to believers, enabling them to rise above sinful patterns of behavior and fulfill divine purposes of righteousness (Rom 8:1-4). Paul also portrays the Spirit as the agency of divine revelation (e.g., 1 Cor 2:10), the source of various gifts (including prophecy, healings, and other exhibitions of divine power) to believers enabling them to contribute to the edification of one another (1 Cor 12:4-11). In other passages, Paul refers to the Spirit as interceding (with "God") on behalf of believers (Rom 8:26-27) and as the divine power working through him in "signs and wonders" and the effectual proclamation of the gospel (Rom 15:18-19; 1 Thess 1:5-6).

This varied and frequent reference to the Spirit is not unique to Paul. For example, Acts also ascribes a varied set of actions that collectively amount to a similar prominence of the Spirit in the narratives of the early churches. As illustrations, in addition to the Spirit filling believers so that they boldly testify to Jesus (4:31; 6:10), the Spirit nudges Philip to engage an Ethiopian eunuch in conversation (8:29) and thereafter snatches Philip off for other duties (8:39). The Spirit alerts Peter to the arrival of men from Cornelius (10:19), directs the church in Antioch (apparently via prophetic oracles) to commission Barnabas and Saul (13:2-4), guides the Jerusalem council to its decision about Gentile converts (15:28), forbids Paul to missionize in Asia (16:6), and warns Paul of trouble in Jerusalem through the prophet Agabus (21:11).

It is particularly noteworthy how many of these NT references involve verbs/actions ascribing a personal agency to the Spirit. In addition to those examples already cited, note also the Markan statement that the Spirit "drove" Jesus into the wilderness (1:12; cf. Matt 4:1/Luke 4:1, where the Spirit "led" Jesus). Or, from the references cited already, recall Paul's portrayal of the Spirit as interceding for believers (Rom 8:26-27), and other passages where the Spirit leads believers and "bears witness" with their own spirits to their filial relationship with "God" (Rom 8:14-16).

In what is perhaps the most sustained focus on the Spirit in the NT, John 14–16, this personal emphasis is clear. Indeed, the repeated use of the distinctive title, *parakletos* (advocate), represents the Spirit as a personal representative of Jesus to be sent to his followers after his departure (e.g., 14:15-16). In this material, the Spirit-Advocate is ascribed the roles of teaching and reminding believers of Jesus (14:25-26), testifying to them on Jesus' behalf (15:26), reproving "the world" for its sin and unbelief (16:7-11), guiding believers into further truth of Jesus' significance, which will involve speaking, declaring "the things that are to come," and glorifying Jesus (16:12-15). I reiterate the point that all these are actions of personal agency, giving the Spirit an intensely personal quality. This frequent use of verbs of agency has the effect of giving the Spirit a considerably more personal character than we find in the OT and the Jewish tradition of the time, in which the Spirit is often referred to in ways that can connote more simply a divine power/force (e.g., 1 Sam 10:9-13).

The Spirit and Eschatology

We have noted that some OT passages prefigure a future time when the Spirit would be more freely dispensed and active and that some NT passages reflect the claim that this hope has been fulfilled in the experiential phenomena ascribed to the Spirit in early Christian circles. The most explicit such passage is, of course, Acts 2:14-21, which as previously noted includes an extended citation of a portion of Joel (2:28-32) that predicts that "in the last days" God will "pour out" the Spirit and that this will signal "the coming of the Lord's great and glorious day." The broad thrust of the sermon ascribed to Peter in Acts 2 is that this prophecy is now fulfilled, that the Spirit is now freely bestowed on those who embrace Jesus as the divinely designated "Lord and Messiah" (Acts 2:36), and that all this means that the "last days" have arrived and so the present is charged with a new eschatological significance.

Indeed, the NT writings collectively reflect a rather evident eschatological orientation, a sense that the authors see believers as living in a time of new divine actions that anticipate and commence a future full redemption of major dimensions. As Dunn noted, "the sect of the Nazarenes was evidently marked out within first-century Judaism by its claim to have been given the Spirit of God in a new and exceptional way."[22] Of course, the ubiquitous NT proclamation that Jesus is "Christ" (Messiah) is itself a claim that he represents and embodies the fulfillment of hopes for a future divine redemption.[23] The point to note here is that the Spirit is often portrayed as a key agent and expression of eschatological developments.[24]

For example, Paul twice refers to the divine bestowal of the Spirit as "the first installment" or down payment (*arrabōn*; 2 Cor 1:22; 5:5; a term used also in Eph 1:13-14), which certainly makes believers' experience of the Spirit the initial stage of an eschatological redemption that will have a much greater future consummation. This is also quite explicit in Romans 8:22-23, where Paul refers to believers as having received "the first fruits [*aparchē*] of the Spirit," a present inward impartation of new divine energy that makes them also long earnestly for the completion of their salvation in "the redemption of our bodies."

The term *first fruits* derives from the practice of sacrifice, in which it designates a portion of an offering made to a deity, but in this unusual metaphorical usage the transaction is reversed; the Spirit is represented as the first stage of a divine gift to believers.[25] The term *arrabōn* derives from the arena of financial transactions and ordinarily designates an initial, partial payment on a larger sum, in this case the present operation of the Spirit in believers portrayed as the initial expression of a redemption that is yet to involve bodily resurrection and bestowal of divine glory on them ("the glory of the children of God," Rom 8:21 NRSV).[26] In fact, the main thrust of Romans 8 is that believers in Jesus now have access to the power of the Spirit to enable the fulfillment of divine righteousness, living "according to the Spirit" (8:4-8, 13), and they are thereby prompted also to set their hope on a further/future redemptive transformation that will include their personal resurrection and glorification (esp. 8:11, 18-23). In Galatians, likewise, Paul urges believers to live and be led by the Spirit in their present lives so as to inherit the kingdom of God in the future (Gal 4:16-18, 21).

This connection of the Spirit and eschatological redemption is also reflected in many other passages in Paul and other NT writers. It is all the more significant that this connection is nowhere expounded but instead is everywhere presumed as an understanding of the Spirit already familiar to readers. Consequently, for example, Paul can simply state that "if you sow to the Spirit, you will reap eternal life from the Spirit" (Gal 6:8) and expect his readers to understand his point. Likewise, in Romans 8:11 (NRSV), Paul's assurance that "he who raised Christ from the dead will give life to your mortal bodies also through his Spirit that dwells in you" presupposes an understanding that Jesus was resurrected through the power of the divine Spirit (e.g., Rom 1:4) and that Jesus' resurrection prefigures the bodily redemption to be bestowed on believers through the same Spirit.

In Hebrews 6:4-5, the author uses a series of likely interrelated expressions to describe believers as those who have been "enlightened, and have tasted the heavenly gift, and have shared in the Holy Spirit, and have tasted the goodness of the word of God and the powers of the age to come" (NRSV). The benefits recited here are probably to be taken as all mutually defining, the experience of the Spirit thus portrayed as a foretaste of the coming consummation. As Attridge observed, these phrases collectively describe "the initial experience of conversion and life in the eschatological community."[27]

Other illustrations of the connection of the Spirit and eschatological hopes are found also in the statements ascribed to John the Baptizer that the coming one whom he announces will baptize with the divine Spirit (Matt 3:11; Luke 3:16). Note also the statement attributed to Jesus that his exorcisms by the Spirit manifest the eschatological arrival of the kingdom of God (Matt 12:28; cf. Luke 11:20).

I trust that it is not necessary to belabor the point further. In the NT, the Spirit (of "God") is typically seen as newly and more richly dispensed, reflecting the eschatological character of the gospel message and the life of believers. The Spirit enables variously new moral endeavor and gifts/powers of ministry (e.g., 1 Cor 12:1-11), all of these things representing incipient manifestations of eschatological blessings that will have still fuller expression in connection with the return of Jesus and the resurrection of the dead. So, the discourse about the Spirit in the NT also reflects an evident excitement. The rich bestowal of the Spirit is both consequence and signal of the inauguration of eschatological redemption.

The Experience of the Spirit

Furthermore, the NT references to the Spirit typically reflect and presuppose experiential phenomena. The Spirit is not simply talked about, and the presence of the Spirit is not simply affirmed as a doctrine; the Spirit is something *experienced*.[28] This is surely another reason for the note of excitement that we find in references to the Spirit in the NT. These texts present the Spirit as a vivid reality in the lives of believers, giving them a strong sense of divine presence and action. For example, Paul's challenge to Galatian believers in Galatians 3:5 seems to presuppose experiential phenomena which they would have understood as manifestations of the Spirit: "Does he who supplies the Spirit to you and works miracles among you do so by works of the law, or by hearing with faith?" (RSV).

In his recollection of missionary activity among the Thessalonian believers, Paul seems to refer to outward phenomena ascribed to the Spirit accompanying his preaching: "our . . . gospel came to you not in word only, but also in power and in the Holy Spirit and with full conviction" (1 Thess 1:5 NRSV). As Paul presents it, this powerful activity of the Spirit enabled the Thessalonians to accept his message, "not as a human word but as what it really is, God's word" (1 Thess 2:13 NRSV). Toward the end of 1 Thessalonians, Paul then also urges the church, "Do not quench the Spirit, do not despise prophesying" (5:19-20). This suggests that he expected that the Spirit was exhibited in particular, outward phenomena that could be discouraged ("quenched") or encouraged.

In 1 Corinthians 2:1-5, Paul claims that he did not rely on rhetorical devices to present himself impressively, but instead his preaching was "with a demonstration of the Spirit and of power, so that your faith might rest not on human wisdom but on the power of God" (NRSV). Here, too, Paul appears to refer to some sort of experiences that he ascribed to the Spirit. Note also Paul's summary of his missionizing work toward the end of his epistle to the Romans, where he refers to Christ working through him "by word and deed, by the power of signs and wonders, by the power of the Holy Spirit" (Rom 15:18-19 RSV). In this statement it appears that the Spirit is the agency by which the "signs and wonders" were wrought. Paul's belief that he is empowered by the Spirit is also likely reflected in his interesting warning that when he came to Corinth again he would put to the test the claims of certain "arrogant people" in the church, "for the kingdom of God does not consist in talk but in power" (1 Cor 4:19-20 RSV).

Moreover, NT texts portray the Spirit's powerful gifts and operations as not confined to apostles but more freely distributed among believers. Paul's extended discussion of various phenomena of the Spirit in 1 Corinthians 12–14 includes a list of various "gifts," each of which is a "manifestation of the Spirit for the common good," including prophecy, utterances of (Spirit-bestowed) wisdom and knowledge, miraculous healings, speaking in tongues, "the working of miracles," and other actions (1 Cor 12:8-10). In this context, Paul presents such "manifestations of the Spirit" as typically operative in the context of gathered worship, and in 14:26 we have his snapshot of this setting as one in which various of these phenomena ("a hymn, a lesson, a revelation, a tongue, or an interpretation") are operative through believers.

Of course, the narratives of Acts likewise portray demonstrative phenomena of the Spirit, such as speaking in tongues (2:3-4; 10:44-47; 19:1-6) and various other miraculous actions ("wonders and signs," 2:43; 4:30; 5:12; 6:8) including healings, exorcisms (e.g., 8:5-8), and prophecy (e.g., 11:27-28; 13:1-3). Indeed, Acts is noted for its emphasis on the Spirit and, in particular, on these outward and dramatic manifestations of the Spirit.[29] Granted, these narratives are likely crafted for dramatic effect and with the intention of presenting the characters in bold colors, and it is not my purpose here to engage adequately historical questions about whether this or that phenomenon actually happened as described, to say nothing of the philosophical and theological issues involved in narratives about miracles. My point in this discussion is simply that the NT rather characteristically presents the Spirit as active and exhibited in phenomena that can be observed and experienced. That is, from the standpoint of the NT authors, the Spirit's activity and power were felt and seen and manifested outwardly in various ways.

Especially in Paul, however, we also have an emphasis on the Spirit as enabling believers in moral life inwardly. Nevertheless, this too is presented as involving powerful experiential phenomena that can be observed in the lives of believers. For example, in a larger context where he deals with various behavioral issues in the Corinthian church, Paul dramatically portrays a major moral transformation of Gentile believers in which the Spirit is operative.

> Do you not know that the unrighteous will not inherit the kingdom of God? Do not be deceived; neither the immoral, nor idolaters, nor adulterers, nor sexual perverts, nor thieves, nor the greedy, nor drunkards, nor revilers, nor robbers will inherit the kingdom of God. And such

were some of you. But you were washed, you were sanctified, you were justified in the name of the Lord Jesus Christ and in the Spirit of our God. (1 Cor 6:9-11 RSV)

In the following verses where he then warns against Corinthian men consorting with prostitutes, Paul presents believers as "united to the Lord" (6:17), their bodies now "a temple of the Holy Spirit," which requires them to exhibit in bodily behavior their new status as redeemed (6:19-20).

Paul's most developed articulations of the Spirit's efficacy in making possible a new life of God-pleasing behavior are in his Epistles to the Galatians and the Romans. For example, in Galatians 5:16-26 Paul urges believers to "walk by the Spirit" (v. 16) and be "led by the Spirit" (v. 18) and "live by the Spirit" (v. 25). Thereby, they will be enabled to desist from "the works of the flesh" (v. 19, defined here with another ad hoc list of sinful behaviors), and to exhibit instead "the fruit of the Spirit" (v. 22, a list of behaviors that seem particularly concerned with interpersonal relations).

But (as is the case with several topics) it is in Romans that we have Paul's most extended statements about the Spirit and the moral transformation of believers. In Romans 6, Paul urges believers to consider themselves effectively "dead to sin and alive to God in Christ Jesus" (6:11 NRSV) and thereby as set free from sin's dominion and enabled now to "become obedient from the heart" (v. 17 NRSV) and so to exhibit God's righteousness and sanctification in their lives (v. 19). Then, in Romans 8, Paul explicitly identifies the divine agency that makes this sort of moral aspiration possible.[30] It is those who live "according to the Spirit" and in whom the Spirit now dwells who are thereby enabled to fulfill "the just requirement of the law" (8:4 NRSV). It is "by the Spirit" that they are to "put to death the deeds of the body" (v. 13).

It seems that for Paul the moral/behavioral transformation that he urged his readers to take seriously involved an operation of the Spirit as powerful as any of the "signs and wonders" that he believed accompanied his ministry. Moreover, the "fruit of the Spirit" (Gal 5:22-23) also carried for him strong eschatological and ecclesiological import as well. Indeed, he portrays the moral power of the Spirit primarily and characteristically in terms of a new enhanced capacity for loving and supportive interpersonal and group relationships. So, the Spirit's enabling of personal "righteousness" both demonstrates and promotes the formation of the *ekklesia* as a circle in which the divine aim of a new (eschatological) humanity marked in personal relationships by *agape* is exhibited.

The Spirit and Jesus

Without doubt, however, the most distinctive and noteworthy feature of the NT references to the Spirit is the strong connection with Jesus. In comparison to the biblical and Jewish tradition of the time, it is simply remarkable for the divine Spirit to be so directly connected with a figure other than "God." Max Turner and his student Mehrdad Fatehi in particular have argued cogently that this has obvious and significant implications in support of what they term a "divine" Christology, Jesus' relationship to the Spirit "best understood after the analogy of the Spirit's relation to God in Judaism."[31] Our focus here, however, is not on Christology but on the effects of the relationship between the Spirit and Jesus upon discourse about "God" in the New Testament.

We may begin by noting some ways in which the activity and experience of the Spirit are linked to the gospel and Jesus. Note, for example, Paul's statement that "no one speaking by the Spirit of God ever says 'Let Jesus be cursed!' and no one can say 'Jesus is Lord' except by the Holy Spirit" (1 Cor 12:3 NRSV). The basic thrust of the statement is that the divine Spirit prompts and enables a genuine recognition and acclamation of Jesus' status as "Lord," which Paul here and elsewhere seems to make the core creedal articulation of Christian faith (esp. Rom 10:9-13; Phil 2:9-11). Indeed, Paul here also seems to make this acclamation of Jesus the key criterion by which in turn one can identify the prompting of the Holy Spirit (as distinguished from the spiritual forces that formerly led the Corinthian Gentiles to worship "idols," v. 2). There is a similar and more explicit statement to the same effect in 1 John 4:1-3: "By this you know the Spirit of God: every spirit that confesses that Jesus Christ has come in the flesh is from God, and every spirit that does not confess Jesus is not from God" (NRSV).

In yet another text, Revelation 19:10 declares that "the testimony of [or to] Jesus is the spirit of prophecy" (NRSV). The import of this saying is, as Swete observed, "To be a true prophet is to witness to Jesus, and to witness to Jesus is to have the prophetic Spirit."[32] We see this connection of the Spirit and prophetic testimony to/about Jesus exhibited elsewhere in the text of Revelation itself. The opening words describe the text as "the revelation of Jesus Christ" (1:1) and a "prophecy" (1:3) that came to the author as he was "in the Spirit" (1:10), i.e., in a special state of inspiration from the divine Spirit.[33] In this state, he has a vision of the glorified Jesus (1:12-20), and the words of Jesus for the seven churches of Asia in 2:1–3:6 are at the same time "what the Spirit is saying to the churches" (3:6 NRSV).

In Paul's discourse about the new situation of believers in Romans 8, it is very interesting to note how he interweaves references to Jesus and the Spirit. He proclaims "no condemnation for those who are in Christ Jesus" (8:1 NRSV) and summons them to live "according to the Spirit" and set their minds on the Spirit (8:4-6). Paul declares that they are "in the Spirit" and indwelt by the Spirit (8:9, 11) and also that "Christ is in you" (8:10). Note further how Paul so easily links references to believers as "justified" and possessing "peace with God through our Lord Jesus Christ" and as those in whose hearts "God's love has been poured . . . through the Holy Spirit" (Rom 5:1-5 NRSV). In Galatians 3:2-5, he insists that the Galatian believers received the Spirit in consequence of their believing the gospel about Jesus proclaimed by Paul, and in a later passage Paul identifies "those who belong to Christ" as summoned and enabled now to live and be guided by the Spirit (Gal 5:24-25).

We can also note again Paul's discussion of the variety of charismatic phenomena in 1 Corinthians 12. Here, he refers to them interchangeably as "gifts" (*charismata*, 12:4), "services" (*diakoniai*, 12:5), and "activities" (*energēmata*, 12:6), all of which reflect or represent the operation of "the same Spirit," "the same Lord [Jesus]," and "the same God." In this passage, we have a very interesting triadic link of "God" with Jesus and the Spirit. The most familiar place where Paul does this, however, is likely the sonorous concluding benediction of 2 Corinthians (13:13 NRSV) where he invokes "the grace of the Lord Jesus Christ, the love of God, and the communion of the Holy Spirit" upon his readers.

The close connection of the Spirit and Jesus is also a recognized emphasis in the Gospel of John (GJohn). In John 7:37-39, the author explains Jesus' statement about "rivers of living water" as anticipating the reception of the Spirit by believers, which would be made available only after Jesus was "glorified." That is, GJohn here makes the bestowal of the Spirit a direct consequence of Jesus' death and resurrection. Then, in narrative fulfillment of this in 20:19-23, the risen Jesus is portrayed as bestowing the Spirit on the disciples (a passage to which I return a bit later in this discussion).

Earlier, in surveying how the Spirit is referred to in very personalized terms in John 14–16, we noted briefly the connection of the Spirit and Jesus. Indeed, these chapters in GJohn form the most extended treatment of the Spirit in the NT, and so I return to this material to emphasize the

Jesus connection. Here, uniquely in the NT, the Spirit is referred to as the "Advocate" (*paraklētos*) to be sent by "the Father" in Jesus' name (14:25) and in consequence of Jesus' departure to heavenly glory and to indwell believers (14:15-17; 16:7). The Spirit is "Advocate" specifically on behalf of Jesus, teaching and reminding believers about Jesus' words (14:25-26), testifying about Jesus to believers (15:26), guiding them "into all the truth" (about Jesus), glorifying Jesus, and declaring Jesus' teachings and significance (16:12-15). The Spirit's advocacy for/of Jesus also extends beyond believers, reproving "the world" for not believing in him (16:8-11). Jesus' role as the "Advocate" on behalf of believers "with the Father" in 1 John 2:1 is complemented in John 14–16 by the Spirit acting as Jesus' "Advocate" on earth.

The Spirit Given by Jesus

It is still more noteworthy that the Spirit of "God" can be referred to as sent or given by Jesus. That is, in some NT texts, Jesus appears to exercise the sort of role in connection with the Spirit that is more typically that of "God." It is not, however, that Jesus is pictured as displacing "God" in this matter. Instead, as with some other divine prerogatives and powers, in NT discourse Jesus shares in God's role in sending and conveying the divine Spirit. Nevertheless, this marks a remarkable innovation in comparison with the ancient Jewish religious matrix in which earliest Christian faith was born. As Max Turner has argued rightly, this authority assigned to Jesus to dispense or send the Spirit is particularly important in reflecting what he calls a "divine christology," Jesus understood as in some real sense participating in the authority and roles of "God."

> *There is simply NO analogy for an exalted human (or any other creature) becoming so integrated with God that such a person may be said to "commission" God's Spirit, and through that to extend that exalted person's own "presence" and activity to people on earth.*[34]

This remarkable innovation is particularly clear in John 14–16. Along with statements in this material that "the Father" will give or send the Spirit-Advocate (14:16, 26), we have other statements that Jesus himself will send the Spirit (15:26; 16:7). In 15:26 there is an interesting link of Jesus and "the Father" in jointly sending forth the Spirit, with Jesus portrayed here as promising the Advocate, "whom I will send to you from the Father, the Spirit of truth who comes from the Father" (NRSV).

A bit earlier in this chapter, I referred to the scene in GJohn where the risen Jesus manifests himself to his disciples and bestows the Holy Spirit upon them (20:21-23) as indicative of the connection made in GJohn between the presence of the Spirit among believers and the completion of Jesus' redemptive work. Let us return to this passage here, however, to underscore its rather direct representation of Jesus as himself imparting the Spirit. Indeed, the reference in this scene to Jesus breathing upon the disciples as he conveys the Spirit seems intended to heighten the point that the "Holy Spirit" (of "God") is at the same time also from and imparted by Jesus.[35]

In the conclusion to Peter's Pentecost speech in Acts 2:29-36, we have yet another NT text making the direct assertion that the risen Jesus now has the authority to bestow the Spirit. After citing Psalm 16 as predictive of Jesus' death and resurrection (Acts 2:24-31), Peter is portrayed as making the following declaration in explanation of the Pentecost phenomenon: "This Jesus God raised up, and of that all of us are witnesses. Being therefore exalted at the right hand of God, and having received from the Father the promise of the Holy Spirit, *he* [Jesus] *has poured out* this that you both see and hear" (Acts 2:32-33 NRSV, emphasis mine).

Also, of course, the prediction ascribed to John the Baptizer in GMatthew and GLuke that the eschatological figure for whom he is precursor will "baptize . . . with the Holy Spirit" (Matt 3:11 NRSV; Luke 3:16) is obviously intended to be taken as pointing to Jesus. This vivid image of baptizing/immersing in the divine Spirit is yet another way in which Jesus is portrayed as exercising a role in regard to the Spirit that is unique and seems more typically that of "God."

The Spirit Identified with Reference to Jesus

This link of Jesus with the Spirit is so strong in NT discourse that the Spirit can sometimes even be identified with direct reference to Jesus. I emphasize again that this is highly unusual in the ancient Jewish context. In fact, it is very difficult to find an instance where the divine Spirit is ascribed in any similar manner to any other figure than "God." This makes the following NT texts striking.

We may commence by noting Galatians 4:4-6. Here, after declaring that in the fullness of time God "sent forth his Son" to accomplish redemption and the adoption of believers as full "sons" of God, Paul then states, "God sent forth the Spirit of his Son into our hearts, crying 'Abba,

Father!' " (Gal 4:6).[36] Not only is the bestowal of the Spirit closely connected with Jesus' redemptive work, the Spirit (of "God") is here also
referred to as "the Spirit of his Son." This remarkable expression is both
unprecedented in Jewish tradition and also unique in Paul, although (as
we shall note shortly) we can find other places where Paul directly identifies the Spirit in connection with Jesus.[37] The basic import of the phrasing here is clearly that the divine Spirit also somehow represents and
conveys the presence of Jesus to believers, making them thereby vividly
aware of their own filial status and that it is patterned after that of Jesus.
In Romans 8:9 we have an equally strong statement. Indeed, in two con-
secutive sentences in this verse, Paul directly refers to the divine Spirit as
also "the Spirit of Christ." "But you are not in the flesh but in the Spirit,
if indeed the Spirit of God dwells in you. But if anyone does not have the
Spirit of Christ, he is not his."

In Philippians 1:19, Paul expresses hope that he will be released from
his imprisonment through the prayers of the Philippian believers "and
the help of the Spirit of Jesus Christ" (*tou pneumatos Iēsou Christou*).
The referent of this interesting phrase must be the divine Spirit (especially given the close contextual connection to prayers), here labeled
"the Spirit of Jesus Christ," as the agency by which Paul understands how
Jesus is made effectually present in his life.[38] That is, the divine Spirit,
more typically presented as the vehicle of the activity and presence of
"God," is here also the means by which the risen Jesus lives and works
in/through Paul.

We have a somewhat similar phrase in the curious account of Paul's
unsuccessful travel plans in Acts 16:6-7. Here we are told that "the Holy
Spirit" forbade him to preach in Roman Asia and then that "the Spirit of
Jesus" likewise prevented him from going into Bithynia.[39] It is most
unlikely that any real distinction is intended. Instead, the author freely
refers to the same divine Spirit by these two expressions, essentially iden-
tifying "the Holy Spirit" as also "the Spirit of Jesus."

In yet another text, the OT prophets are portrayed as inspired by "the
Spirit of Christ within them" to testify prophetically to "the sufferings
destined for Christ and the subsequent glory" (1 Pet 1:11 NRSV). In the
next verse, the author refers to "the Holy Spirit sent from heaven" (1:12)
as the inspiring force behind the proclamation of the gospel to the readers. Here also we have the divine Spirit identified with reference to Jesus.
Effectively, these texts as well present a kind of double identity of the
Spirit.

The close connection of the Spirit and Jesus is reflected in another text that has presented special difficulties for interpreters, 2 Corinthians 3:15-18. Because of these difficulties, any proposal about the meaning of the passage requires some extended discussion. In the preceding verses, Paul declares that the gospel represents a new "dispensation of the Spirit," which supersedes the "dispensation of death, carved in letters of stone," an obvious allusion to the Torah given through Moses. Paul then commences an innovative appropriation of the Exodus 34 story of how Moses veiled his face (which shone from being irradiated with divine glory) when speaking with the Israelites. Paul contends that the unfortunate effect of Moses' action was to prevent the Israelites from seeing that the glory of Moses' revelation was temporary, a fading splendor (3:12-13), which Paul makes indicative of the provisional nature of the Torah, now superseded by the "new covenant" (3:6) based on Jesus' work and significance. Paul then makes Moses' veil a metaphor for contemporary Jewish unbelief toward the gospel, claiming "that same veil" lies over their hearts, impeding a proper perception and response, "for only in Christ is [the veil] taken away" (3:14). Then come the statements with which we are concerned here.

> But to this day, whenever Moses is read a veil lies over their heart; but whenever one turns to the Lord the veil is removed. Now "the Lord" is the Spirit, and where the Spirit of the Lord is, there is freedom. And we all, with unveiled face, beholding the glory of the Lord, are being changed into the same likeness [*eikona*] . . . as from the Lord, the Spirit [*kyriou pneumatos*]. (3:15-18)

The particular exegetical questions relevant for us are whether "the Lord" in 3:16-17 is Jesus, and, if so, what kind of relationship of the Spirit and Jesus Paul intends to posit here. On the first question, although an impressive case has been offered for taking "the Lord" in 3:16-17 as referring to "God" (*Yahweh*) or even the Spirit, I incline to the view that (as is Paul's dominant usage of *Kyrios*) the reference is to the risen/glorified Jesus.[40] Note particularly, just a bit later in the larger context, Paul's three-word summary of what he advocates: "Jesus Christ (as) Lord" [*Iēsoun Christon Kyrion*, 4:5]. Moreover, surely in 3:18 (NRSV), Paul's statement about believers "seeing the glory of the Lord as though reflected in a mirror" and being changed thereby must refer to a transformative apprehension of Jesus' divine significance. Granted, Paul credits this revelatory work to the Spirit ("as from the Lord, the Spirit," 3:18).

But in the larger context (especially 3:12–4:10), his main concern seems to be to underscore the cognitive shift involved in the recognition of Jesus' glorified/glorious status by fellow Jews (in 3:7-18) and among the wider public (in 4:1-6).

But what, then, shall we make of Paul's statement, "the Lord is the Spirit," in 3:17? The first thing to note is that this statement is closely linked to the immediately preceding one about the illumination that comes when a person turns to "the Lord" (3:16). In this creative adaptation of the statement in Exodus 34:34 that "whenever Moses went in before the LORD . . . he would take the veil off," Paul vividly likens Christian conversion as a turning to "the Lord" and the cognitive effect that results as the removal of a veil from the heart.[41] If "the Lord" in 3:16 is Jesus, in v. 17 Paul emphasizes that this Lord reveals himself through and is disclosed effectually by the Spirit.[42] Then Paul posits that "the Lord, the Spirit" (3:18) enables people to perceive with devotion "the glory of the Lord [Jesus]" and be changed thereby "into his likeness."[43]

This view of Paul's referent in 3:15-18 accords with Paul's statement earlier (3:1-3) that the Corinthian believers are "a letter of Christ, prepared by us, written not with ink but with the Spirit of the living God." Paul here pictures Jesus as the author of these epistles of the heart, with Paul and the divine Spirit the media through which they are composed.

In short, I think it best to see 3:15-18 as reflecting Paul's profound conviction about the close connection of the Spirit and Jesus. This connection is such that "the Spirit of the Lord" (3:17) is the means by which Jesus is revealed as glorious to believers and also how Jesus is powerfully present in their lives. This does not involve a flat identification of Jesus and the Spirit, however. The unique phrase, "the Lord is the Spirit," certainly striking and memorable, is indicative of a remarkably close link; but the larger context of Paul's references to the risen Jesus and the Spirit makes it clear that for Paul they are fully distinguishable and yet also intimately related. Fatehi proposed that Paul's link of the Spirit and the risen Jesus should be understood as "a *dynamic identification*," the Spirit acting to communicate Jesus' presence, power, and glory to believers and Jesus in some real way "actually present and active through the Spirit."[44] This seems to me to be a cogent characterization.

To note another striking phrase from another Pauline passage, even when Paul says, "The first man, Adam, became a living soul; the last

Adam became a life-giving spirit" (1 Cor 15:45 NRSV), this should not be taken to mean that Jesus and the divine Spirit are simply merged into one entity. Instead, this is another instance of Paul's vivid ways of positing (here echoing vv. 21-22) that, in contrast with the mortality inherited from Adam, the risen Jesus now has Spirit-power to give (resurrection) life, i.e., power indicative of Jesus' postresurrection role as the dispenser of the divine Spirit.[45]

As we approach the end of this discussion of how the Spirit and Jesus are related in the NT, it is appropriate to note that there are phrases here and there in biblical and extracanonical Jewish texts that at first glance may appear to be precedents and analogies. But in fact none of them really involves the same sort of reidentification of the divine Spirit that we have in NT texts.[46] For example, in 2 Kings 2:15, we read of "the spirit of Elijah" resting upon Elisha, which seems to be a reference to the gift of prophetic inspiration manifested in Elijah, with Elisha portrayed as being given a similar prophetic gift. Philo uses the expression "the Spirit of Moses" (*to Mōuseōs pneuma*, Gig. 24) in commenting on the account in Numbers 11:24-25 where "the LORD . . . took some of the spirit that was on [Moses] and put it on the seventy elders; and . . . they prophesied" (NRSV). Philo emphasizes that this is the divine Spirit, not Moses' human spirit (*Gig.* 26-27), but here also the expression "Spirit of Moses" seems simply Philo's way of saying that the elders were given the same prophetic gift that Moses had. In the rabbinic text *Genesis Rabbah* (2:4), we find the phrase "the Spirit of the Messiah," likely referring to the divine Spirit's anointing of the Messiah. In short, none of these really provides an analogy or explanation for the way that the divine Spirit comes to be so closely identified with reference to Jesus in NT texts. In particular, none of these other texts portray the divine Spirit as dispensed by these figures.

As indicated earlier, the christological implications of the close association of Jesus and the Spirit are significant, and these have been the focus in most of the recent discussions of these texts. But my aim here is to highlight how in these NT texts discourse about the divine Spirit is shaped by this link with Jesus. This remarkable link of the Spirit with Jesus reflects a significant development in discourse about "God," the divine Spirit bearing now a double identity as agent and mode of the presence and activity of "God" and serving in very similar ways also on behalf of the risen Jesus.

SUMMARY

In summary, I want to highlight two main emphases demonstrated in this chapter. First, in NT discourse about "God," the Spirit is very prominent. Indeed, granting readily that NT references to the Spirit draw upon biblical and ancient Jewish tradition, the place of the Spirit in NT discourse is markedly greater.

Moreover, NT texts seem to reflect a rich and vibrant body of religious experiences attributed to the Spirit. That is, for the sort of early Christians reflected in NT texts, "God" is not simply a subject for contemplation and discourse but is described as *experienced* with an immediacy and impact in their lives. This experience of "God" is ascribed to the Spirit. To be sure, "God" can also be described in terms that emphasize transcendence and otherness, as in 1 Timothy 6:16: "It is [God] alone who has immortality and dwells in unapproachable light, whom no one has ever seen or can see; to him be honor and eternal dominion" (NRSV). But for early believers this only made the sense of divine presence and activity in their lives and gathered worship all the more thrilling. In their outlook, the Spirit directly and powerfully conveyed this august and transcendent "God" to and in them.

Furthermore, they portray their experiences of the Spirit as a foretaste and confirmation of eschatological hopes and signs that full redemption is near. This contributes to the excitement that one detects in the NT references to the bestowal of the Spirit.

My second emphasis is that various NT references to the Spirit posit a distinctive link also with Jesus, which in turn gives a distinctive triadic shape to NT discourse about "God." That is, in NT discourse about "God" the Spirit is notably prominent, and in NT discourse about the divine Spirit, a link with Jesus is also notable. In the concluding reflections to this book, I explore further what this triadic shape to NT discourse about "God" represents.

C H A P T E R   F I V E

CONCLUDING OBSERVATIONS

DIVERSITY AND COHERENCE

In the foregoing chapters, we have focused on several key questions to do with "God" in the New Testament, and I have taken a somewhat synthesizing approach in the handling of NT evidence. Nevertheless, I hope to have reflected adequately some of the particularities of various NT texts. But some readers may well press further the question of whether the diversity in the NT really permits us to treat this body of writings in the way I have. So, the first topic I want to address further here is that question. I have reserved direct consideration of it for this final chapter for two reasons. My first reason is because it seemed more important to present what the NT texts have to say and let readers judge whether there was sufficient coherence, the proof of any pudding being in the tasting. My second reason is that my discussion in defense of the approach taken in the book will be relatively brief. In my view, essentially, the differences among NT texts on "God" have to do more with emphases, not radical or incompatible differences; there is a fundamental coherence and agreement in key matters. In the introduction to this book, I briefly indicated this, and in what follows I provide some further support and illustrations for my judgment.

Perhaps the most ready illustration is in how NT texts refer to "God" as "Father," the most commonly used epithet for "God" in the NT.[1] As we noted in chapter 2, such references appear in various NT authors/texts, and yet there are also interesting particularities of emphasis among them. In what follows I take up the matter again and discuss some of these particularities a bit further. Unavoidably, this will involve some occasional repetition of observations from previous chapters.

Among the Gospels, for example, Father-language for "God" is particularly frequent in GMatthew and GJohn. In GMatthew this frequency is deployed especially to emphasize that God is "Father" for Jesus' followers as well as for Jesus.[2] With a distinctive frequency, in GMatthew Jesus repeatedly refers to "your Father" when speaking to his disciples (e.g., 5:16, 45, 48; 6:1, 4, 6, 8, 14, 15, 18, 26, 32; 7:11; 10:20) in sayings that encourage them (and the intended readers) to look trustingly to their "heavenly Father" and live in relationship to him. That is, the frequency of reference to God as "Father" in Matthew seems particularly intended to serve what we may call the pastoral concerns of the author. In GJohn, however, references to God as "Father" appear still more frequently but function mainly in support of the Johannine christological emphasis that Jesus is the unique "Son" of "the Father," and so has unique authority. Consequently, in GJohn Jesus is pictured as referring to "the Father" (i.e., particularly *Jesus'* "Father") frequently in dialogues and debates with nondisciples (e.g., 3:35; 5:17, 18, 20-23, 26, 36-37, 43).

Nevertheless, it is clear that both GMatthew and GJohn draw upon and develop what was already a traditional Christian way of referring to "God." Indeed, in our earliest extant Christian texts, Paul's letters (which are commonly thought to be some twenty years or more earlier than the Gospels), "Father" is already a familiar way that believers refer to and address "God" in prayer/worship (e.g., 1 Thess 1:2-3; 3:11-13). Moreover, this reference to "God" as "Father" is reflected also in GMark (8:38; 11:25; 13:32; 14:36) and GLuke (e.g., 6:36; 9:26; 10:21-22; 11:2). So, neither GMatthew nor GJohn asserts something radically new or different in their respective emphases on God as "Father." Instead, each of them deploys "Father" language for a particular purpose or emphasis, whether a more pastoral one (GMatthew) or a christological/polemical one (GJohn).

Similarly, "the God and Father of our Lord Jesus Christ," though apparently deriving from Paul (Rom 15:6; 2 Cor 1:3; 11:31; Eph 1:3; and taken up also in 1 Pet 1:3), reflects a christological conviction (Jesus' special filial status) and a claim about "God" (as having authorized and exalted Jesus) that seems to have been rather commonly shared among early Christian circles. In other passages, Paul can refer to "our God and

Father" (e.g., 1 Thess 3:11; Phil 1:2), which means that for Paul, too, although "God" is "Father" to Jesus in a unique way, believers also are brought into a filial relationship with this God through Jesus.

To take yet another example of other particularities in the discourse about "God" in NT writings, I turn to Hebrews. In this important text there is an emphasis that "God" is the deity attested in the OT, to whom devout personages of biblical tradition entrusted themselves (esp. Hebrews 11). Also the author's distinctively strong cultic/sacrificial motif portrays "God" as having appointed Jesus to a unique priestly status and as recipient of Jesus' priestly service (e.g., 2:17; 3:1-6; 5:5-10; 7:26-28; 8:1-7; 9:13-14, 23-28). Yet, although these themes are presented with distinctive emphasis in Hebrews, they are neither unique to this text nor in conflict with what other NT texts have to say about "God." For example, Paul too refers to "God" and Jesus' redemptive work in cultic/sacrificial terms (e.g., Rom 3:21-26) and even portrays Jesus as priestly intercessor (Rom 8:34).

In Revelation there is still another distinctive emphasis on God as "the one who sits on the throne" in heaven, the all-powerful cosmic ruler (e.g., 1:4; 4:2, 9-10; 5:1, 7, 13; 6:16; 7:10, 15; 19:4; 21:5). The reason behind this particular imagery and emphasis seems to be the author's concern to assert, over against what he regards as the blasphemous claims of the Roman imperial regime, that it is really this "God" who is the true and rightful ruler and the sole one to whom full allegiance is to be given (e.g., 11:15; 14:6-7; 19:10). Indeed, in Revelation there is also a particularly notable emphasis that proper worship of and allegiance to "God" includes Jesus ("the Lamb") as well, the divinely authorized co-recipient (e.g., 5:9-14; 7:10, 15-17).[3] Yet, fully granting these distinctive emphases in Revelation, we must also note that in this text, too, we have a particular deployment of fundamental convictions that were rather widely shared in Christian circles of the time. The ideas that "God" is the true heavenly ruler who trumps all earthly claims of sovereignty and that Jesus holds a uniquely exalted position with "God" in heaven and in Christian devotional practice were hardly either innovations of this author or in tension with the beliefs of other believers.

We could consider further instances of particular emphases in God-discourse in other NT texts, but I can think of none that would really represent a radical difference in beliefs. I certainly do not wish to mask or unduly minimize the rich variety in emphases in discourse about "God" among the NT writings. Nor do I intend any disparagement or lack of appreciation for scholarly studies that focus on particular authors or texts and discuss more thoroughly their particular emphases about "God." Instead, I simply wish to underscore the view developed and illustrated in earlier chapters that in basic beliefs about "God," the NT texts actually cohere quite well.

If we simply compare NT texts with one another, the distinguishing emphases are apparent and interesting. But if we compare any of the NT texts with some other early Christian writings that genuinely exhibit the more radical diversity of beliefs about "God" that characterized Christianity in the second and third centuries, it will become clear that the corpus that constitutes the NT reflects a broadly shared standpoint on the matter.

This is readily demonstrated in the point made in chapter 2 that in all the NT texts, the "God" affirmed is the deity proclaimed in the writings that constitute what came to be the Christian OT. This deity is the sole creator of all things, the supreme heavenly ruler of the cosmos for whom no cult-image is appropriate (or at least not the usual kind) and to whom alone among the other deities of the religious environment cultic worship is to be offered. In the NT texts, "God" is the God of Abraham, Isaac, and Jacob, the deity who gave the Torah through Moses, the God of ancient Israel, and in relation to whom Jesus' own significance and status is presented. This deity is at once both transcendent and distinguishable from all of creation and even from other putatively divine beings and yet is also revealed through the biblical prophets and, most fully, in Jesus. I really do not think that any NT text challenges these ideas or presents what amounts to a significantly different outlook.

On the other hand, as we have noted earlier in this book, in figures such as Marcion and in the so-called gnostic texts (that represent what Michael Williams prefers to call "biblical demiurgical traditions") we have early Christians of very different outlooks and very different discourses about "God."[4] For Marcion, the OT deity was an inferior being, and the true God was previously unknown before Jesus declared him. For so-called gnostics, the OT creator-deity was an evil figure, a tyrant who falsely claimed to be the sole deity. They hoped to be released from the world of sense and matter (the imprisoning domain of the tyrannical creator-god) to be joined with the ultimate deity (variously referred to, e.g., as the "unknown Father," "Abyss," "the God who is not") in the realm of transcendent light. Unquestionably, there was radical diversity in early Christianity, perhaps particularly so in the second century.

Indeed, this radical diversity makes it all the more obvious and interesting that the God-discourse reflected in the NT texts exhibits a clear coherence and obvious agreement in fundamentals.

So, along with scholarly studies that focus on the distinguishing emphases of particular authors/texts, I trust that it is entirely appropriate to have taken the approach laid out in this book. Dunn may be correct in insisting that the unity of the NT is a "unity in diversity."[5] But, at least on discourse about "God," I contend that the NT writings exhibit a profound unity and that their diversity is relatively minor in comparison. To cite a musical metaphor, the NT texts do not play in unison. But the diversity in the NT texts in discourse about "God" may be compared to a lively jazz combo with a number of participants, each of whom can deliver his or her own "take" on the common melody. I certainly hope that the discussion in the preceding chapters has demonstrated that the NT is an essentially coherent corpus in relation to the questions posed in these chapters.

THE TRIADIC SHAPE OF GOD-DISCOURSE IN THE NT

The other important matter to which I return for further reflections here is what I have called the triadic nature of God-discourse in the NT.[6] That is, NT discourse about "God" typically also includes references to Jesus and the Spirit. To be sure, there are continuing disagreements among scholars over precisely how Jesus' exalted status and significance were understood in this or that NT text and over exactly how the Spirit and the risen Jesus were understood in relation to each other. On the first question, Maurice Casey, for example, contends that Jesus did not really become fully divine in early Christian thought and practice until late in the first century and that the earliest evidence of this is in GJohn.[7] Though disagreeing with Casey on some points, Dunn takes a similar view of the timeframe in which Jesus came to be regarded as in some genuine sense divine. Both Casey and Dunn insist that in Paul's Epistles in particular (ca. 50–65 C.E.), Jesus is not yet treated as genuinely divine or the recipient of worship.[8] In several publications, however, with a number of other scholars, I have argued that devotion to Jesus as in some real and unique sense partaking in divine attributes and powers erupted very quickly and quite early—so early that it is all presupposed in Paul's letters written within twenty to thirty years after Jesus' execution.[9] I have proposed that the devotional pattern reflected already in Paul's letters amounts to a distinctive "mutation" in Jewish monotheistic practice, in which Jesus features in an unprecedented way in worship directed to "God." In particular, the pattern of devotional practices reflected in the NT, in which devotion to "God" programmatically involves Jesus, effectively links Jesus with "God" in a manner that is simply unique in comparison to all known expressions of Jewish piety of the time. That is, Jesus is regarded in these texts as linked with "God" in an unprecedented manner, such that worship of "God" must now also involve Jesus.[10]

But whatever view one takes on the meaning of the clear and remarkable devotion given to Jesus in Paul, it is indisputable that from our earliest extant NT texts (Paul's letters) onward, early Christian discourse about "God" characteristically also refers to Jesus as bearing a unique significance. Indeed, it is not too much to say that one cannot adequately speak of "God" in the NT without including reference to Jesus. References to the Spirit are also frequent, although perhaps not quite as central in the NT as a corpus.

Of course, it would be anachronistic to ascribe the developed doctrine of the Trinity to any writer in (or as early as) the NT texts. For example, discussions about a divine "substance" shared by "persons" of the Trinity come later, as second- and third-century Christian thinkers drew upon and adapted philosophical categories.[11] But the point I want to underline here is that these later discussions were made unavoidable (at least for Christians of the "proto-orthodox" circles for whom the Christian traditions reflected in the NT were important) by the prior triadic shape of discourse about "God," which we see richly attested already in the NT texts. That is, the NT writings vigorously affirm the "one God" stance inherited from the Jewish matrix of earliest Christian faith but also (and with at least equal vigor) affirm especially the nonnegotiable significance of Jesus in belief and devotional practice, and further, frequently refer to the divine Spirit as the mode or agency by which "God" and Jesus are made present and real to believers. So, the question of how to harmonize these affirmations, particularly how to posit "one God" genuinely and yet also recognize Jesus as somehow really sharing in divine glory, could not be avoided by Christians in the second and third centuries C.E.

It is, however, interesting to note that, although this triadic nature of NT God-discourse required serious and sustained theological reflection, especially in the second century C.E., it has often been ignored or distorted in some forms of popular Christianity, from the early centuries down to the present time (as noted briefly in chapter 2). In some of these cases, Jesus is treated simplistically as all there is to "God," effectively overwriting "God the Father," especially in devotional practice. So, for example, in these forms of Christian piety, prayer and worship are directed simply to Jesus, typically without any reference to "the Father."[12] This is quite different from the more typical devotional pattern reflected in the NT texts of prayers usually addressed to "the Father" through or in the name of Jesus and cultic reverence given to Jesus as obedience to "God." Indeed, as demonstrated in earlier chapters, in the discourse and devotional practices reflected in the NT generally, Jesus' divine/glorious significance is typically articulated with reference to "God" ("the Father"). So, for example, in 2 Corinthians 4:4-6, Paul refers to Jesus as "the image [*eikōn*] of God" and to believers as enabled to perceive "the knowledge of the glory of God in the face of Jesus Christ."

My main concern here, however, is not to engage these particular expressions of ancient or modern popular Christian piety in which Jesus effectively eclipses "God." Nevertheless, I do want to add that the triadic nature of NT God-discourse also reflects relatively stable/fixed relationships ascribed to the trio involved. So, for example, in various NT texts we have statements that "God" ("the Father") sent forth Jesus, gave him over to death, raised him from death, exalted him to heavenly glory, appointed him to act as eschatological judge, gave him power to raise the dead, and established him as rightful recipient of universal acclamation and the cultic devotion of believers. That is, Jesus is rather consistently pictured as functioning in subordination and obedience to "God" ("the Father"), and the reverse is never stated.

Likewise, the Spirit is pictured as sent forth by "God" (and in some texts by Jesus) but never the opposite.[13] Moreover, Jesus is consistently the one whose redemptive actions form the subject of gospel proclamation. The Spirit is referred to typically as empowering this proclamation and accompanying it with "signs and wonders" and more generally stimulating belief and acceptance of the message proclaimed. But the Spirit is not the subject or content of the proclamation; Jesus is.

This triadic-shaped discourse surely also reflects the shape of the religious experiences of the Christian circles reflected and addressed in the NT writings. As others have observed previously, these early Christians experienced what they took to be the God of the biblical (OT) traditions acting newly and decisively in and through Jesus. They experienced Jesus as in some unprecedented way the expression of divine revelation and redemptive purposes. Indeed, they experienced Jesus as risen from the dead, exalted to heavenly glory, and powerfully operative in their circles, perhaps especially in the corporate worship setting. They ascribed these experiences to the "Holy Spirit" working in and upon them, the divine Spirit sent into and among them as the gift and medium of divine presence. They also experienced the presence and power of the risen Jesus in and through what they took to be the operations or manifestations of the Spirit. As Fee observed in his study of Pauline letters, "Paul's experience of Christ and the Spirit caused him to think of the 'one God' in terms that included the Son and the Spirit."[14]

Of course, the relationship between the beliefs and the experiences involved in all this is complex, perhaps even moreso given that we are considering beliefs and experiences shared and circulated in groups and in a culture and time far removed from today. I intend no naive view of things, and it is not my purpose here to explore the psychological, social, or philosophical questions that could be directed at this matter. But, whatever one makes of these sorts of experiences of early Christians, there can be little doubt that they had experiences that they understood in these religious terms. That is, the sort of "God"-discourse that we have in the NT did not arise from philosophical reflection and academic impulses. It was not initiated as an intellectual exercise to address some problem of metaphysics or to stake out some novel position in the spectrum of religious thought of the day. Instead, the triadic contours of discourse about "God" in the NT reflect the "triangular" shape of early Christian religious experience in which "God," Jesus, and the Spirit featured as linked in the special ways we have observed.[15]

I repeat that the triadic discourse about "God" in the NT is not the developed trinitarian doctrine of subsequent centuries, but equally, I contend that the latter would not have developed without the "God"-discourse and the devotional pattern that we find attested in the NT. There is not the space here to justify the contention, but I trust that little justification is required for anyone acquainted with the early trinitarian developments. One illustration will suffice. However much Justin Martyr drew upon Platonic and Stoic ideas and/or prior Jewish appropriation of these traditions (as, e.g., in Philo of Alexandria), it is clear that the major impulses driving his efforts to develop and defend his faith were convictions and devotional practices such as those already reflected in the NT.[16]

In hindsight, therefore, should we regard the NT discourse about

"God" as an embryonic stage of the developed doctrine of the Trinity? Of course, the specifics of that later doctrinal development also owe much to other factors, such as philosophical categories of the time and perhaps even political theory of the late second and third centuries about plurality and unity in the imperial office.[17] Also, we should not imagine that the authors of NT texts saw their beliefs as embryonic of further doctrinal developments, which they obviously could not have anticipated. That is, they did not likely regard their beliefs as preliminary stages to some more developed statement of things, certainly not the specific developments of the patristic period. Moreover, even posing the question in these terms could suggest some concern about (or challenge to) the legitimacy of the subsequent trinitarian doctrinal development, but it is not primarily my objective to address this sort of issue here. Instead, I simply underscore the point that a historical approach to the development of trinitarian doctrine in the patristic period requires us to recognize that it did not take place "out of the blue" but to a large extent as a consequence of profound religious convictions and devotional practices that we observe already in the NT texts. I contend that the major factor was the inclusion of Jesus as a distinguishable figure along with "God" in early Christian devotion, producing the question of how to combine this with an exclusivist "monotheistic" stance. Certainly, Christian efforts to understand who and what "God" is in light of Jesus' divine significance in particular did not commence in the second century C.E. but with the beliefs and devotional phenomena that we find in the NT.

So, would it be going too far to think of the NT texts as reflecting what we might call a "proto-Trinitarian" outlook? Among contemporary scholars, perhaps Gordon Fee has been most emphatic in this claim, especially with reference to Paul's letters.[18] From his massive study of Paul's references to the Spirit, Fee judged that "Paul expresses his experience of God in a fundamentally Trinitarian way, but never grapples with the theological issues that this experience raises."[19] A few pages later, Fee refers to "the plain and certain Trinitarian texts" in Paul and insists that "Paul's understanding of God was functionally Trinitarian."[20] Indeed, in his analysis of passages such as 1 Corinthians 12:4-6, Fee even states, "Thus the Trinity is presuppositional to the entire argument."[21] Granting that Paul's concern in references to "God," Jesus, and the Spirit was not "ontological (= the nature of their *being* God), but soteriological (= their role in salvation)—and experiential," Fee nevertheless insists that in a number of Paul's statements about salvation (and the experience of it) "we meet the Trinity in Paul."[22] Fee also characterizes Paul's thought as "functionally Trinitarian," and insists that "this soteriological Trinitarianism is foundational to Paul's understanding of the gospel," citing a number of passages where Paul refers to the respective roles of God, Jesus, and the Spirit in salvation.[23]

In a book published originally in 1962 and curiously often overlooked today, Arthur Wainwright also directly addressed the question. He contended that although the *doctrine* of the Trinity is not stated formally in the NT there is evidence that "the *problem* of the Trinity was in the minds of certain New Testament writers, and that they made an attempt to answer it."[24] As Wainwright distinguished the terms, a "doctrine" represents an answer to a theological "problem." Wainwright defined "the problem of the Trinity" as prompted "because Christians believed that Jesus was divine," and they expressed this belief "both in the writings of the New Testament and in the worship which was practised by the earliest Christian communities." Because early Christians also dominantly "upheld the Jewish belief in the unity of God, the belief in Christ's divinity raised a serious problem." How could "the Father" and Jesus both be treated as divine "and yet God be one?"[25] Granting readily that in the second century C.E. and thereafter Christian efforts to grapple with the problem of the Trinity "became more and more systematized"; he nevertheless insisted, "New Testament writers were aware of the trinitarian problem and made an attempt to answer it," although in the NT texts "it is easier to see the first attempts to clarify the problem than the first attempts to answer it."[26]

It is, of course, technically a verbal anachronism to use the word *Trinity* in discussions of NT texts, for the word and the elaboration of the many issues involved appeared in subsequent centuries. But, equally, it would be historically simplistic to disconnect these later developments from the phenomena of NT beliefs and devotional practices that we have analyzed in this book. So, Wainwright was correct in probing the connections and also, in my view, in contending that in NT texts we see earlier evidence that Christians recognized the basics of "the problem" involved.

Wainwright was also perceptive in emphasizing the importance of worship practices as evidence of how Jesus had come to complicate (if I may use the term) the question of "God" for believers, already in the first century C.E.

> The problem of the Trinity was from the beginning closely connected
> with Christian worship. It was not the concern of the scholar alone, but

was a vital issue for the worshipping Christian. . . . The nature of Christian worship influenced the development of Christian thought, and, conversely, the development of thought influenced the nature of worship. Such an interplay of thought and worship helps to explain the emergence of the problem of the Trinity.[27]

As we have seen (especially in chapter 3), the devotional practices reflected in the NT constitute significant evidence, particularly for taking stock of the place of Jesus in the religious outlook and life of the circles reflected in these texts.

It is interesting that, although "God" and Jesus feature much more as the recipients of Christian devotional practice in NT texts, the religious discourse in these texts typically involves reference to "God," Jesus, and the Spirit. In previous publications I have referred to the "binitarian" pattern or shape of devotional practice (worship) in the NT, in which "God" and Jesus are thematized and invoked.[28] I intend no surreptitious projection of later ideas back into NT texts in characterizing the devotional pattern in them as "binitarian." The word is simply an attempt to capture the fact that these texts evidence a novel (at the historical point of its origin) pattern of devotion in which "God" and Jesus feature as distinguishable and yet uniquely linked subjects and recipients of reverence in the setting of corporate worship. So, regardless of what one thinks of the term, it is really the phenomena of NT devotional practice that are the issue. To use a colloquialism, there is an undeniable "two-ishness" to the devotional life reflected in the NT, however one understands the specific beliefs about Jesus vis-à-vis "God."

But the discussion in the preceding chapters has shown that if we focus on the *discourse* about divine actions in NT writings a "three-ishness" is readily apparent, with frequent references to "God," Jesus, and the divine Spirit. So, to come back to the question posed a bit earlier, how should we regard this triadic-shaped discourse about "God" in the NT? Does it amount to a "proto-Trinitarian" discourse? Is "the problem of the Trinity" already emergent and addressed in the NT?

As Wainwright rightly observed, "The central problem of the Trinity is that of the divinity of Christ and the relationship of Christ to the Father."[29] Certainly, in historical terms the originating issue that led to what Wainwright called "the problem of the Trinity" was how to reconcile the intense devotion to Jesus reflected already in the earliest NT texts with the profession that "God" is one. So, what are the indications that NT authors were aware of this as a real or potential problem?

It is remarkable that the intense Jesus-devotion reflected in Paul's letters, which constitute our earliest extant Christian writings, is more presupposed than expounded and that there is scarcely any extended
justification offered for treating Jesus in such a reverential manner. One
might suppose that Paul's Gentile converts may not have been troubled
by any "monotheistic" scruple and so might not have found devotion to
Jesus any problem in itself. After all, in the larger religious environment
of the time there were deities and demigods aplenty. But in view of his
devout (Pharisaic) Jewish background, it is difficult to imagine that Paul
would not have detected any potential tension with the core Jewish profession of "one God." One might also wonder whether Jewish believers in
Roman Judea would have accepted this sort of Jesus-devotion if it had
been shaped by pagan religious ideas or had emerged in Gentile Christian
circles.[30]

Wainwright recognized these difficulties but simply accepted Bousset's
claim that Paul came around to an acceptance of Jesus' divine status
under the influence of anonymous "Hellenistic Christians" during his
sojourn in Damascus and Arabia after his conversion experience.[31]
Bousset's claim, however, that this devotion to Jesus could not have characterized Jewish believers in Roman Judea and must have arisen in dias-
pora settings influenced by a pagan religious outlook always rested more
on assertion than evidence.[32] More recent studies of Paul and of the historical evidence lead to a very different view of things.[33] In sum, it
appears that the sort of Jesus-devotion reflected in Paul's letters *was*
shared among Jewish believers in Roman Judea as well as among Paul's
churches. So, how did devout Jewish believers embrace this place of Jesus
in belief and practice and see it as compatible with their traditional faith
in "one God"? And why is there so little indication that this is an issue in
Paul's letters between him and Judean/Jewish believers?

To take the latter question first, it is important to remember that Paul's
letters were addressed to circles of converted believers, not to outsiders.
These historically invaluable writings were not intended to persuade people to embrace Christian faith but instead presuppose a Christian commitment shared between Paul and his addressees. There are, of course,
issues on which Paul seeks to correct his readers, but these are entirely
concerned with a right understanding of some things and, perhaps even
more often, with what Paul regarded as the right behavioral consequences
of their shared faith. So, if there is scant justification for devotion to Jesus
presented in these texts, the most likely reason is that it was not under

dispute between Paul and his Christian addressees. Moreover, it is likely that it was not under dispute between Paul and Jewish believers in Jerusalem or elsewhere. There were differences between Paul and some other Jewish believers, to be sure, for Paul was rather forthright in declaring them (e.g., Gal 1:6-9; 2:4-5, 11-14; 2 Cor 11:1-23). Essentially, these differences concerned the validity of Paul's Gentile mission and the terms on which Gentile converts could be treated as full coreligionists by Jewish believers. Given Paul's open statements about differences with some other Jewish believers, therefore, it is all the more significant that Jesus-devotion never features among the issues disputed.

But I propose that we do have indications of the bases on which Paul and other early believers of his time offered devotion to Jesus. These are briefly stated and, it appears, reflect convictions already traditional among believers by the time of Paul's letters. Behind these somewhat formulaic statements there must lie some profound convictions and a radical new understanding of divine purposes that would have required some major cognitive shifts, especially for those believers from a traditional Jewish background. A few illustrative examples of what I refer to will suffice.

One of these brief formulaic statements appears in Romans 1:3-4, which declares that Jesus was raised from death and declared to be "the Son of God" through the exercise of divine power. The key point in this statement is that Jesus' unique status (note the definite article: "*the* Son of God") is his by divine action. "God" raised him and declared his exalted place. In Philippians 2:9-11 we have a somewhat fuller statement (though still more formulaic than discursive), where Jesus' supreme title ("the name above every name") and exalted position over all creation are declared to have been conferred by "God the Father," who thereby has mandated a universal acclamation of Jesus as "Lord."

In both of these texts we have illustrations of the basic conviction that Jesus' status in belief and in devotional practice rests upon the actions and authority of "God." I contend that this conviction functioned for earliest believers such as Paul as the basis and justification for the noteworthy devotion to Jesus that Paul affirmed. Indeed, that "God" had declared Jesus' high status meant more than a justification for reverencing him; it constituted a *requirement* to do so. This is probably the implication of the statement in Philippians 2:11 that the divinely intended universal acclamation of Jesus as "Lord" was "to the glory of God the Father." This in turn means that any refusal of devotion to Jesus would amount to disobedience to "God."

I propose that such brief statements as we have considered here express the sort of convictions and rationale that lay behind Jesus-devotion for earliest believers, including especially Jewish believers. Essentially, they were convinced that "God" had exalted Jesus to a unique status and now demanded that he be reverenced in recognition of this divine action. Nevertheless, in that ancient Jewish setting this was a remarkable idea. I repeat for emphasis that in these statements we probably have the daring answer to the crucial question posed above concerning how Jewish believers felt able to reconcile their remarkable devotion to Jesus with their traditional commitment to "one God."

But, to put it mildly, it is clear that these sorts of claims did not always carry much force with other Jews. In my view, it is understandable, therefore, that the zealous Pharisee, Saul, initially felt obliged to "destroy" the new religious movement among fellow Jews in which Jesus featured with such prominence (Gal 1:13-14) and that he required some considerable time for reflection after the remarkable revelatory experience that commenced his dramatic reorientation from opponent to advocate of Jesus and the young Christian movement (Gal 1:15-17).[34] Paul refers to a divine "revelation," the core content of which was the startling recognition of Jesus' unique status as the unique "Son" of the God whom he thought he had been serving in his efforts against Jesus-followers (Gal 1:15-16). Certainly, something about these early believers struck Saul as sufficiently outrageous and threatening to the religious integrity of Jewish tradition as to require his vigorous actions of persecution. I suggest that other scholarly suggestions that Saul was angered by a perceived laxness in Torah observance or criticism of the Jerusalem Temple, perhaps especially among "Hellenistic" Jewish believers, are not as well-founded as some have supposed.[35]

It is probably in GJohn, however, that we have the most explicit indications that there was a "problem" in this devotion to Jesus, especially from the standpoint of the larger Jewish community and the concern about "one God." But it would be a mistake to think that the major reason for this is that the issue had not developed earlier. There are plenty of indications that Jesus-devotion generated opposition among some Jewish circles from the earliest years and onward and so would have required Jewish Christians to present some justification for their religious stance.[36] The likely reason that we see more obvious references to Jewish critiques of Jesus-devotion in GJohn is that this writing was intended more directly to advocate and reaffirm Christian belief, especially in the face of these Jewish critiques. Indeed, it is commonly thought among scholars that GJohn bears the marks of a bitter polemic between Jewish believers and hostile Jewish religious leaders that led to these believers being expelled from their larger Jewish community.[37] Further, I contend that the most likely explanation for their expulsion is that their claims for and devotion to Jesus were deemed outrageous and unacceptable by their fellow Jews. Whether one takes the explicit statement of purpose in 20:30-31 as evangelistic ("that you may come to believe") or as the reassurance of believers ("that you may continue to believe"), GJohn clearly gives a robust, even combative, affirmation of Jesus-devotion over against unbelief, especially Jewish unbelief in Jesus.[38]

Various passages peculiar to GJohn, though set in the narrative time of Jesus, likely reflect the polemics between Jewish believers and critics in the larger Jewish community.[39] As examples, note the accusations in 5:18 that Jesus was "making himself equal to God," and in 10:33 that Jesus blasphemed "because you, though only a human being, are making yourself God [or a god]." The statement ascribed to Jesus in 5:22-23 seems to me more likely to reflect the sort of justifying claim that Jewish believers gave for their devotion to Jesus in the "post-Easter" period: "The Father judges no one but has given all judgment to the Son, so that all may honor the Son just as they honor the Father. Anyone who does not honor the Son does not honor the Father who sent him" (NRSV).

In any event, these passages do likely show that the "problem" posed by Jesus-devotion for the traditional Jewish monotheistic stance had surfaced, likely a long time previous to the composition of GJohn, and had to be engaged by believers. So, given that this issue was the historical core and origin of what became "the problem of the Trinity," Wainwright was correct to judge that at least in GJohn we have explicit indication that first-century believers already were required to frame some rationale for what Jewish critics saw as their problematic religious stance. GJohn is still a long way from the developed doctrine of the Trinity, but it is not too much to see in this text clear evidence of the prior emergence of the "problem" to which that doctrine was the intended answer.

But I want to emphasize that we should not view the NT discourse about "God" simply as some early and preliminary stage of later and mature developments. Even though there is a historical connection between the ideas and discourse about "God" in the NT and doctrinal developments of subsequent centuries, I urge that the NT texts deserve to be heard in their own right. I think that it is patronizing, even demeaning, to treat them as representing preliminary and immature expressions of faith. The discourse about "God" in these texts was, for NT authors and their intended readers, as serious and as worthy of study for its own sake as anything that came later. Indeed, I submit that in historical terms NT "God" discourse is the more remarkable and innovative than subsequent developments. The NT texts use different terms and categories than later trinitarian doctrine, but that should not justify any view that their discourse about "God" is historically or theologically inferior and subordinate to later doctrinal expressions.

THE GOD OF THE NT IN HISTORICAL PERSPECTIVE

In chapter 2, I emphasized the particularity of the God affirmed in the NT in the context of the Roman era, and I want to comment a bit further on the matter as we near the end of this study. Essentially, I wish to draw attention to the larger history-of-religions significance of "God" as portrayed in the NT. I think that the historical significance of NT God-discourse may not have been adequately recognized. Indeed, I would go as far as to claim that in the NT we have what amounts to a historically significant critique of popular ideas of the time about "gods" and a notable innovation in religious belief and practice. The absence of Christian temples, images, altars, and sacrifice, and the rejection of the whole cafeteria of Roman-era deities (except, of course, for the OT deity, at least among "proto-orthodox" Christians) all surely amount to a quite distinguishable stance for the time. It is all the more interesting that this represents a critique of religion and the gods from a *religious* standpoint. That is, in the name of what they believed is the true deity they leveled a radical critique against almost the entire religious outlook of their day. In fact, so radical was their stance in the eyes of many contemporaries that Christians came to be accused of "atheism," an impious rejection of the gods.[40]

Granted, that charge had been made earlier against Socrates; and devout Jews had rejected the deities of the pantheon long before the earliest Christians. Moreover, as noted in chapter 2 briefly, even among some pagan philosophers there were critiques of animal sacrifice and a more transcendent view of the ultimate deity. But I also repeat for emphasis that there is little evidence that these philosophical musings had any significant impact on popular religious practice (or that there was any such intention). It is one thing to bandy about an idea in the dining circles of self-styled sophisticates; it is quite another to set out to change belief and behavior at large. As for Jewish refusal to worship the gods, this seems in general to have been regarded simply as an ethnic peculiarity of Jews, something a bit offensive but tolerable usually (as Romans tended in general to tolerate the peculiarities of the various peoples of the empire).

Early Christianity, however, represented a vigorously evangelistic movement that sought to win adherents from among the general public, translocally and transethnically, and succeeded in doing so. Consequently, the Christian critique of the gods and religion had much more potential for causing trouble for the religious establishment. Also, given that in the Roman era what we call "religion" involved social relations and even had political significance, the religious stance advocated already in the NT had profound implications in these dimensions of life as well. The early Christian religious standpoint was not simply the topic of polite discussion in elite dining settings but was propounded as integral to the Christian movement in the streets, homes, shops, courts, and other settings in which believers affirmed their faith. Indeed, I propose that early Christianity constituted the first popularly based critique of the gods and religion in the ancient Roman world (and remained the only one until the rise of Islam several centuries later).

Even in comparison with the Jewish religious matrix in which earliest Christianity emerged, there are both strong connections and also significant developments reflected in the patterns of God-discourse and religious devotion attested in the NT. Particularly in the uniquely central place of Jesus in reference to "God" and in the practice of devotion to "God" that is presumed in the NT, we have a major innovation. Indeed, from the standpoint of at least some devout Jews of the time (and subsequently), this amounts to a departure from the tradition that may even constitute a violation of the first commandment to preserve the uniqueness of "God." So, one could even ask whether the God of the NT is the Jewish God.

As we have seen, on the one hand, the NT texts are consistent in claiming that it is the God of the OT, the God of Jewish tradition, who sent Jesus, raised him from death, and exalted him to heavenly glory, and now demands that Jesus be reverenced. On the other hand, these same texts emphasize that in view of these things it is now no longer possible to speak adequately of "God" without confessing Jesus' significance and, equally important, that an adequate obedience and devotion to "God" now requires the inclusion of Jesus as recipient of reverence and devotion with "God." So, the NT texts express a major reconfiguring of God-discourse, and a major reconfiguring of devotion to "God" as well.

These important developments took place within a remarkably brief time span, so brief that the NT texts already presuppose them. As noted a number of times already, in subsequent centuries the beliefs and religious practices reflected in the NT generated further developments in Christian doctrine and devotional life. But, simply as the remarkable developments in the history of religions that they are, the NT expressions of beliefs about "God" deserve attention.

They also deserve attention by theologians, indeed, by any Christian. The NT texts are not (in the main) theological treatises or systematic reflections on the faith that they reflect.[41] These writings will, therefore, require a readiness by theological readers to adjust their thought processes to the more ad-hoc presentation of religious truths that we find in the NT and to texts that more often presuppose beliefs and so refer to them in brief summary form rather than explicating them. Moreover, they do not use some of the vocabulary of later doctrinal discussions about "God," such as talk about divine "substance" and divine "persons." Instead, for example, we have references to Jesus sharing divine "glory" and the divine name and being seated with "God" in heavenly exaltation/enthronement. In any case, it would be wise to avoid reading the NT texts through the lens of theological issues and controversies of later times. To engage the NT appropriately will require theologians to acquire some sense of what the terms and conceptual categories used in *these* texts meant. But this may in turn provide theologians with fresh resources for thinking about "God." Indeed, they may well find resources that will enable creative formulation of theological questions and fresh perspectives on them.

Although it takes me outside of my usual sphere of comfort to engage the sort of topic more typical of systematic theologians, I will dare to offer an example of what I mean. I suggest that the NT texts offer a body of discourse that presents a more dynamic view of "God," with the focus on divine actions rather than the more static categories of philosophically influenced theology of later centuries. For example, the emphasis in the NT on the resurrected and exalted Jesus might have profound implications for traditional views of divine immutability. If, as the NT texts seem to insist, discourse about "God" now must include reference to Jesus, then this marks a significant alteration from the way that "God" was understood previously. In particular, Jesus' resurrection constitutes the emphatic reaffirmation of Jesus (and precisely as the embodied human figure) as thereafter uniquely to be included in the understanding of divine purposes and even (per traditional trinitarian faith) in what is meant by "God." To use trinitarian language, "God the Son" is eternal, without beginning or end. But in the incarnation "the Son" became genuinely an embodied human, and in Jesus' resurrection this incarnate move was irrevocably reaffirmed by "God." In short, from Jesus' resurrection onward, "God" in some profound way now includes a glorified human. That, I believe, represents quite a significant alteration!

The biblical texts typically taken as reflecting the idea of divine immutability (e.g., Num 23:19; Ps 46:1-3; 102:25-28; Jas 1:17; Heb 13:8) all seem to emphasize what we may call a *moral* immutability, i.e., divine trustworthiness. But NT theological discourse seems to posit interesting developments that involve "God" as well as creation. Furthermore, this more dynamic view of "God" may well have profound implications for other theological themes, such as how "salvation" is understood. If the resurrected/glorified Jesus is the exemplar and pathfinder for the full salvation to be given to believers (e.g., Rom 8:12-25, 28-30), then a breathtaking vista opens on what this salvation comprises.

Systematic theologians more adequately prepared to consider such matters will likely be able to take any such proposal much further (and perhaps offer some corrections or objections to my brief sketch above). But my point is that a serious engagement with NT discourse about "God" is worth the effort involved. If this slim volume contributes to that engagement, I will be pleased.

NOTES

Introduction

1. Nils Alstrup Dahl, "The Neglected Factor in New Testament Theology," *Reflections* 75 (1975): 5–8; reprinted in Nils Alstrup Dahl, *Jesus the Christ: The Historical Origins of Christological Doctrine* (ed. Donald H. Juel; Minneapolis: Fortress Press, 1991), 153–63. I cite the latter publication here from p. 154.

2. Larry W. Hurtado, "God," *DJG*, 270–76.

3. Dahl, *Jesus the Christ*, 155–56.

4. Oscar Cullmann, *The Christology of the New Testament* (trans. Shirley C. Guthrie and Charles A. M. Hall; Philadelphia: Westminster Press, 1963 [German 1957]), 2–3.

5. Dahl, *Jesus the Christ*, 154.

6. I shall have more to say about this in a subsequent chapter.

7. Andreas Lindemann, "Die Rede von Gott in der paulinische Theologie," *TGl* 69 (1979): 357–76 (359).

8. E. P. Sanders, *Paul and Palestinian Judaism* (Philadelphia: Fortress Press; London: SCM, 1977), 509, cited in Neil Richardson, *Paul's Language about God* (JSNTSup99; Sheffield: Sheffield Academic, 1994), 16.

9. Cf., e.g., James D. G. Dunn, *New Testament Theology: An Introduction* (Nashville: Abingdon Press, 2009), 38–39.

10. Ibid., 38.

11. On the "new atheism" espoused, e.g., by Richard Dawkins and others prominent in recent years, see the fine critical engagement by my colleague David Fergusson, *Faith and Its Critics: A Conversation* (Oxford: Oxford University Press, 2009).

12. See Dunn's discussion of questions about a focus on canonical texts in the volumes in this series: *New Testament Theology*, 4–6.

1. "God" in/and New Testament Scholarship

1. In her recent large study of terms used for God in the NT, Christiane Zimmermann likewise referred to "a certain new awareness of the theme of God" in NT scholarship since the 1970s. *Die Namen des Vaters: Studien zu ausgewälten neutestamentlichen Gottesbezeichnungen vor ihrem frühjüdischen und paganen Sprachhorizont* (AJEC 69; Leiden: Brill, 2007): 4.

2. Nils Alstrup Dahl, *Jesus the Christ: The Historical Origins of Christological Doctrine* (ed. Donald H. Juel; Minneapolis: Fortress Press, 1991), 158–59.

3. For a review of some recent major works on NT theology, see C. Kavin Rowe, "New Testament Theology: The Revival of a Discipline. A Review of Recent Contributions to the Field," *JBL* 125 (2006): 393–419.

4. Halvor Moxnes, *Theology in Conflict: Studies in Paul's Understanding of God in Romans* (NovTSup; Leiden: Brill, 1980), 5.

5. Dahl, *Jesus the Christ*, 157.

6. Paul-Gerhard Klumbies, *Die Rede von Gott bei Paulus in ihrem zeitgeschichtlichen Kontext* (Göttingen: Vandenhoeck & Ruprecht, 1992), 11–12.

7. Ibid., 243, 250–51.

8. Ibid., 246–47.

9. Ibid., 252.

10. Neil Richardson, *Paul's Language about God* (JSNTSup 99; Sheffield: Sheffield Academic Press, 1994), 12–18, citations from 18. It is unfortunate that Richardson's study makes no reference to Klumbies's book.

11. Ibid., 312.

12. Ibid., 18.

13. Ibid., 88.

14. Ibid., 90.

15. Ibid., 312.

16. Ibid., 312–13.

17. Ibid., 311. For his full discussion, see 240–56.

18. Ibid., 241.

19. Ibid., 307.

20. Larry J. Kreitzer, *Jesus and God in Paul's Eschatology* (JSNTSup 19; Sheffield, U.K.: JSOT Press, 1987).

21. Cf. Kreitzer, e.g., 23–29; Richardson, 273–88.

22. Richardson, *Paul's Language*, 315.

23. Gordon D. Fee, *God's Empowering Presence: The Holy Spirit in the Letters of Paul* (Peabody, Mass.: Hendrickson, 1994), 6.

24. Ibid., 898.

25. Ibid.

26. James D. G. Dunn, *The Theology of Paul the Apostle* (Edinburgh: T & T Clark; Grand Rapids: Eerdmans, 1998).

27. Ibid., 47, 49.

28. Ibid., 29.

29. Ibid., 28–29.

30. Ibid., 29.

31. Dunn's discussion of Paul's christology comprises pp. 163–315, and his comments on Christ as "fulcrum" are pp. 722–29 of *Theology of Paul*.

32. These phrases are all from Dunn, *Theology of Paul*, 722–23.

33. Ibid., 727. In the remainder of the sentence cited in part here, Dunn adds "just as he envisaged Gentiles not knowing the law but being the law for themselves," likely an allusion to Rom 2:14-16. But with a number of other scholars, I take these verses to refer to Gentile *Christians*, who do not "by nature" have the law but are enabled to meet the righteous demand of the Torah through the effects of the gospel in their lives. See, e.g., Simon J. Gathercole, "A

Law unto Themselves: The Gentiles in Rom 2.14-15 Revisited," *JSNT* 85 (2000): 27–49. In this view, Paul does not envision non-Christian Gentiles having God's favor apart from Christ.

34. Francis Watson, "The Triune Divine Identity: Reflections on Pauline God-Language, in Disagreement with J. D. G. Dunn," *JSNT* 80 (2000), 99–124.

35. Ibid., 99 n. 1, and cf. 104.

36. Ibid., 104–5.

37. Ibid., 106.

38. Ibid., 110.

39. Ibid.

40. Citing the heading of the section of Watson's article beginning on 111.

41. Ibid. He also cites (114 n. 23) a similar statement by Neil Richardson (*Paul's Language*, 307).

42. Ibid., 119–23.

43. Ibid., 121–22.

44. Ibid., 123.

45. Donald Guthrie and R. P. Martin, "God," *DPL*, 354–69.

46. Ibid., 367.

47. Ibid.

48. To distinguish the Gospels as texts from their putative authors, I refer to them as "GMatthew," "GMark," etc.

49. John R. Donahue, "A Neglected Factor in the Theology of Mark," *JBL* 101 (1982): 563–94.

50. Ibid., 594.

51. François Vouga, "Habt Glauben an Gott. Der Theozentrismus der Verkündigung des Evangeliums und des christlichen Glaubens im Markusevangelium," in *Texts and Contexts: Biblical Texts in Their Textual and Situational Contexts. Essays in Honor of Lars Hartman* (ed. Tord Fornberg and David Hellholm; Oslo: Scandinavian Universities Press, 1995), 93–109.

52. Klaus Scholtissek, "Er ist nicht ein Gott der Toten, sondern der Lebenden (Mk 12,27). Grundzüge markinischer Theologie," in *Der lebendige Gott. Studien zur Theologie des Neuen Testaments: Festschrift für Wilhelm Thüsing zum 75* (ed. Thomas Söding; Münster: Aschendorf, 1996), 71–100.

53. Paul Danove, "The Narrative Function of Mark's Chracterization of God," *NovT* 43 (2001): 12–30.

54. Ibid., 25.

55. Ibid., 26.

56. Ibid., 30.

57. Jack Dean Kingsbury, " 'God' within the Narrative World of Mark," in *The Forgotten God: Perspectives in Biblical Theology* (ed. A. Andrew Das and Frank J. Matera; Louisville: Westminster John Knox, 2002), 75–89.

58. Ibid., 79.

59. Ibid., 80.

60. C. Drew Smith, " 'This Is My Beloved Son: Listen to Him': Theology and Christology in the Gospel of Mark," *HBT* 24 (2002): 53–86. The article arose from Smith's Edinburgh PhD thesis, "The Theology of the Gospel of Mark: A Literary-Theological Investigation into the Presentation of God in the Second Gospel" (2004), which, unfortunately, has not been published.

61. Smith, "Beloved Son," 84.

62. Ibid., 86.

63. Gudrun Guttenberger, *Die Gottesvorstellung im Markusevangelium* (BZNW 123; Berlin: Walter de Gruyter, 2004).

64. Ibid., 162. See her fuller discussion of Mark's view of Torah in the light of Mark's historical context, 165–82.

65. Ibid., 217, and 285–87.

66. Ibid., 331–32, 333.

67. Ibid., 335.

68. R. L. Mowery, "God, Lord and Father: The Theology of the Gospel of Matthew," *BR* 33 (1988): 24–36.

69. A. Andrew Das and Frank J. Matera, eds., *The Forgotten God: Perspectives in Biblical Theology* (Louisville: Westminster John Knox, 2002). The volume has essays on Mark, Luke-Acts, John, Romans and Galatians, the Corinthian Epistles, Colossians and Ephesians, the Pastoral Epistles, Hebrews, James and the Petrine Epistles, and Revelation, plus four more essays on "God" in various parts of the Old Testament.

70. Mowery, "God, Lord and Father," 24.

71. Robert L. Brawley, *Centering on God: Method and Message in Luke-Acts* (Louisville: Westminster John Knox, 1990).

72. John T. Carroll, "The God of Israel and the Salvation of the Nations," in Das and Matera, *Forgotten God*, 91–106, quotation from 91.

73. Diane G. Chen, *God as Father in Luke-Acts* (StBL 92; Bern/Frankfurt: Peter Lang, 2006). This work originated as a PhD thesis written under Marianne Meye Thompson's supervision at Fuller Theological Seminary.

74. C. K. Barrett, "Christocentric or Theocentric? Observations on the Theological Method of the Fourth Gospel," in *Essays on John* (London: SPCK, 1982), 1–18.

75. Paul W. Meyer, " 'The Father': The Presentation of God in the Fourth Gospel," in *Exploring the Gospel of John: In Honor of D. Moody Smith* (ed. R. Alan Culpepper and C. Clifton Black; Louisville: Westminster/John Knox, 1996), 255–73, quotation from 259.

76. Francis J. Moloney, "Telling God's Story: The Fourth Gospel," in Das and Matera, *Forgotten God*, 107–22, quotation from 107–8.

77. Tord Larsson, *God in the Fourth Gospel: A Hermeneutical Discussion of the History of Interpretation* (Coniectanea Biblica, NT Series 35; Lund: Almqvist & Wiksell, 2001).

78. Marianne Meye Thompson, *The God of the Gospel of John* (Grand Rapids: Eerdmans, 2001).

79. Ibid., 14–15. Note also, e.g., C. K. Barrett, " 'The Father is greater than I' (John 14.28): Subordinationist Christology in the New Testament," in *Essays on John* (Philadelphia: Westminster, 1982), 246, "There could hardly be a more Christocentric writer than John, yet his very Christocentricity is theocentric" (cited by Thompson, *God of the Gospel of John*, 239).

80. Thompson, *God of the Gospel of John*, 51.

81. Ibid., 240.

82. Note also Paul N. Anderson, "The Having-Sent-Me Father: Aspects of Agency, Encounter, and Irony in the Johannine Father-Son Relationship," *Semeia* 85 (1999): 33–57.

83. I omit some items such as Edgar Krentz, "God in the New Testament," in *Our Naming of God* (ed. C. E. Braaten; Minneapolis: Fortress, 1989), 75–90.

84. James M. Reese, "The Principal Model of God in the New Testament," *BTB* 8 (1978): 126–31, quotation from 128.

85. Ibid., 128–29.

86. Ibid., 129.

87. Neil Richardson, *God in the New Testament* (Peterborough: Epworth, 1999).

88. Ibid., 9.

89. Ibid., 52.

90. Ibid., 59.

91. Christfried Böttrich, "Die neutestamentliche Rede von Gott im Spiegel der Gottesprädikationen," *BTZ* 1 (1999): 59–80.

92. Ibid., 77–78 (translation mine).

93. Zimmermann, *Die Names des Vaters*.

94. Marianne Meye Thompson, *The Promise of the Father: Jesus and God in the New Testament* (Louisville: Westminster/John Knox, 2000).

95. Ibid., 21–34 (reviewing the debate about Jeremias's claims), and 35–55 (her own study of Jesus' use of "Father" language for God).

96. Ibid., 156.

97. Ibid., esp. 158–72.

98. Ibid., 19.

99. Jerome H. Neyrey, *Render to God: New Testament Understandings of the Divine* (Minneapolis: Fortress, 2004).

100. See somewhat similar reservations expressed in a review of Neyrey's book by Richard M. Edwards, *RBL* 05/2005.

101. E.g., in addition to my own contribution on "God" in the Gospels mentioned earlier (n. 2 of the Introduction) and the article by Guthrie and Martin on Paul (n. 45 above), see Carey C. Newman, "God," *DLNT*, 412–31; and Jouette Bassler, "God in the NT," *ABD* 2:1049–55.

102. James D. G. Dunn, *New Testament Theology: An Introduction* (Nashville: Abingdon Press, 2009), 41–69. The main body of Dunn's discussion focuses on "The Inherited *Theo-logy*" (beliefs from the OT/Jewish tradition, 43–53) and "Making Sense of Jesus (Christology) in Relation to Theo-logy" (53–67).

103. I take the term from Böttrich's opening sentence of his essay (59): "Die Gotteslehre scheint eher ein Stiefkind der ntl. Theologie zu sein."

2. Who Is "God" in the New Testament?

1. I quote part of the definition from the Wikipedia entry on "God": http://en.wikipedia.org/wiki/God. Though not to be treated uncritically as a source for assured scholarship, it is surely one of the best witnesses to *popular* understanding of matters such as this.

2. E.g., S. R. F. Price, "Gods and Emperors: The Greek Language of the Roman Imperial Cult," *JHS* 104 (1984): 79–95, concisely shows the breadth of what the Greek word *theos* designated.

3. Polymnia Athanassiadi and Michael Frede, eds., *Pagan Monotheism in Late Antiquity* (Oxford: Clarendon, 1999); cf. John A. North, "Pagans, Polytheists and the Pendulum," in *The Spread of Christianity in the First Four Centuries: Essays in Explanation* (ed. William V. Harris; Leiden: Brill, 2005), 125–45.

4. See, e.g., Robert M. Grant, *The Gods and the One God* (Philadelphia: Westminster, 1986); Larry W. Hurtado, "First Century Jewish Monotheism," *JSNT* 71 (1998): 3–26, republished in L. W. Hurtado, *How on Earth Did Jesus Become a God? Historical Questions about Earliest Devotion to Jesus* (Grand Rapids: Eerdmans, 2005), 111–33. To be sure, ancient Jewish texts also reflect the reference to other heavenly beings (e.g., angels) as "gods" or "sons of God," but the application of these epithets to such beings did not entail the legitimacy of worshiping them. So, there remained a firm practical distinction between what *god* meant when applied to such beings and when used to refer to the one deity, *YHWH*, to whom alone cultic worship should be given.

5. Paul's discussion of things pertaining to idolatry is particularly in 1 Cor 8 and 10. Paul's defense of his apostolic rights and his behavior in 1 Cor 9 seems to interrupt this discussion. Gordon Fee proposed that it may have been triggered by Corinthian questions about his own authority and consistency in such matters. Gordon D. Fee, *The First Epistle to the Corinthians* (NICNT; Grand Rapids: Eerdmans, 1987), 392–94.

6. In ordinary ancient Greek usage, *eidōlon* typically had the neutral meaning "image" or "phantom" (as a phantom of a dead person).

7. I have discussed these matters further in *How on Earth Did Jesus Become a God?* 56–82.

8. Elizabeth A. Castelli, "Imperial Reimaginings of Christian Origins: Epic in Prudentius' Poem for the Martyr Eulalia," in *Reimagining Christian Origins: A Colloquium Honoring Burton L. Mack* (ed. Elizabeth A. Castelli and Hal Taussig; Valley Forge, Pa.: Trinity Press International, 1996), 173–84, quotation from 179.

9. F. Gerald Downing, *God with Everything: The Divine in the Discourse of the First Christian Century* (Sheffield: Sheffield Phoenix, 2008), esp. chs. 3–4, compares theological ideas of the pagan philosopher Dio Chrysostom and Paul.

10. Indeed, one of the charges hurled against Christians on account of their refusal to worship the traditional deities was that they were atheists, e.g., *Mart. Pol.* 3:2; 9:2.

11. Hendrik F. Stander, "Marcion," *EEC*, 715–17; Sebastian Moll, "Marcion: A New Perspective on His Life, Theology, and Impact," *ExpTim* 121 (2010): 281–86; L. W. Hurtado, *Lord Jesus Christ: Devotion to Jesus in Earliest Christianity* (Grand Rapids: Eerdmans, 2003), 549–58.

12. Nils A. Dahl, "The Arrogant Archon and the Lewd Sophia: Jewish Traditions in Gnostic Revolt," in *Sethian Gnosticism* (vol. 2 of *The Rediscovery of Gnosticism*; ed. Bentley Layton; Leiden: Brill, 1981), 689–712, discusses how gnostic texts used OT texts such as Isaiah 43:10 as arrogant claims by the tyrant demiurge deity.

13. Michael A. Williams, *Rethinking "Gnosticism": An Argument for Dismantling a Dubious Category* (Princeton: Princeton University Press, 1996), esp. 51–53; Simone Pétrement, *A Separate God: The Christian Origins of Gnosticism* (trans. Carol Harrison; San Francisco: HarperSanFrancisco, 1990 [French 1984]), 29–50; Alistair Logan, *Gnostic Truth and Christian Heresy* (Edinburgh: T & T Clark, 1996), esp. 71–116.

14. Tertullian (ca. 160–230 C.E), *Against Marcion* (*Adversus Marcionem*), a five-book work written in successive editions 205–213 C.E. English translation: ANF 3:269–474.

15. Justin Martyr, *1 Apology*. English translation: ANF 1:159–87.

16. Note, e.g., Psalm 78, which opens (vv. 1-4) with the emphasis on declaring "the deeds of the LORD" as the mode by which knowledge of God is to be communicated to successive generations.

17. See, e.g., the various prayers to pagan deities included in Mark Kiley, ed., *Prayer from Alexander to Constantine: A Critical Anthology* (London: Routledge, 1997), 123–204.

18. See, e.g., Werner Beierwaltes, "The Love of Beauty and the Love of God," in *Classical Mediterranean Spirituality* (ed. A. H. Armstrong; New York: Crossroad, 1986), 293–313.

19. Some statistics: The typical NT word translated "love," *agapē*, is used 116 times, and the verb *agapaō* another 143 times, illustrative of how important these terms are in NT vocabulary. In many of these cases the words are in sentences referring to the love of "God."

20. See esp. Marianne Meye Thompson, *The Promise of the Father: Jesus and God in the New Testament* (Louisville: Westminster John Knox, 2000).

21. "Our Father who is in heaven" (*avinu sh^e-bashamayim*) is found in prayers that form part of the traditional "Morning Service." On reference to God as "Father" in rabbinic tradition, see George Foot Moore, *Judaism in the First Centuries of the Christian Era* (Cambridge, Mass.: Harvard University Press, 1927–30), 2:201–11.

22. I draw here upon my discussion of God in the Gospels in L. W. Hurtado, "God," in *DJG*, 270–76.

23. See, e.g., Larry W. Hurtado, "Jesus' Divine Sonship in Paul's Epistle to the Romans," in *Romans and the People of God* (ed. Sven K. Soderlund and N. T. Wright; Grand Rapids: Eerdmans, 1999), 217–33.

24. Of course, to modern ears "sons" may seem uncomfortably male-oriented. The intended emphasis, however, is that the privileges of sons in the ancient culture are conveyed to all believers, male and female.

25. Gordon J. Bahr, "The Use of the Lord's Prayer in the Primitive Church," *JBL* 84 (1965): 153–59; G. J. Bahr, *The Lord's Prayer and Jewish Liturgy* (New York: Seabury, 1978), 149–55.

26. G. W. E. Nickelsburg, *Resurrection, Immortality, and Eternal Life in Intertestamental Judaism and Early Christianity* (HTS 56; expanded ed.; Cambridge, Mass.: Harvard Divinity School, 2006); Alan F. Segal, *Life after Death: A History of the Afterlife in Western Religion* (New York: Doubleday, 2004), 248–81.

27. E.g., L. W. Hurtado, *One God, One Lord: Early Christian Devotion and Ancient Jewish Monotheism* (2d ed.; London: T & T Clark, 1998; orig. ed., 1988), 93–124; idem, *At the Origins of Christian Worship* (Carlisle, England: Paternoster, 1999; Grand Rapids: Eerdmans, 2000), 63–97.

28. It is not entirely clear whether the author of GJohn understood Isaiah 6 as a vision of the future glorification of Jesus or as a vision of the "preincarnate" Jesus. On the importance of the vision in Isaiah 6 in early Christianity, see Darrell D. Hannah, "Isaiah's Vision in the Ascension of Isaiah and the Early Church," *JTS* 50 (1999): 80–101.

29. See esp. John R. Levison, *The Spirit in First-Century Judaism* (AGJU 29; Leiden: Brill, 1997).

30. J. D. G. Dunn, *Jesus and the Spirit: A Study of the Religious and Charismatic Experience of Jesus and the First Christians as Reflected in the New Testament* (London: SCM; Philadelphia: Fortress, 1975).

31. Max Turner, *Lord of the Spirit: Monotheism, Christology, and Trinitarian Worship in the New Testament* (Milton Keynes, England: Paternoster, 2007).

32. See, e.g., R. P. C. Hanson, *The Search for the Christian Doctrine of God: The Arian Controversy* (Edinburgh: T & T Clark, 1988); and Eric Osborn, *The Emergence of Christian Theology* (Cambridge: Cambridge University Press, 1993).

3. "God" and Jesus in the New Testament

1. Arthur Cushman McGiffert, *The God of the Early Christians* (Edinburgh: T & T Clark, 1924).

2. See J. Gresham Machen's lengthy review on McGiffert's book: "The God of the Early Christians," *PTR* 22 (1924): 544–88.

3. Joseph Jungmann noted the much higher frequency of prayers to Jesus in Christian apocryphal literature, suggesting that these writings reflected forms of early "popular" Christian piety as distinguished from the more Trinitarian prayer practices promoted by church leadership in corporate worship settings. *The Place of Christ in Liturgical Prayer* (2d rev. ed.; London/Dublin: Geoffrey Chapman, 1965), 165–68. But cf. now Paul Bradshaw's critique of Jungmann's view: "God, Christ, and the Holy Spirit in Early Christian Praying," *The Place of Christ in Liturgical Prayer: Trinity, Christology, and Liturgical Theology* (ed. Bryan D. Spinks; Collegeville, Minn.; Liturgical Press, 2008), 51–64. In the same volume, Baby Varghese describes prayers to Jesus in Syrian liturgical texts: "Prayers Addressed to Christ in the West Syrian Tradition," 88–111.

4. See the interesting study of the most frequently used "contemporary" Christian worship music: Lester Ruth, "Lex Amandi, Lex Orandi: The Trinity in the Most-Used Contemporary Christian Worship Songs," in Spinks, *Place of Christ in Liturgical Prayer*, 342–59. Also, there are Christians who explicitly deny the Trinitarian view of God and contend that Jesus is the name of God and that "Father," "Son," and "Holy Spirit" are simply modes or aspects of Jesus. See David A. Reed, *"In Jesus' Name": The History and Beliefs of Oneness Pentecostals* (JPSSup; Blandford Forum: Deo Publishing, 2008).

5. E.g., in an edition of the Greek NT on my desk that gives solely the text with no critical apparatus, the four Gospels comprise 217 pages of a total of 480 pages, roughly 45 percent.

6. "Call upon" translates here *epikaleō*, which in the Greek OT can designate worship/invocation of a deity. E.g., W. Kirchschläger, "ἐπικαλέω," *EDNT* 2:28–29.

7. See, e.g., L. W. Hurtado, *One God, One Lord: Early Christian Devotion and Ancient Jewish Monotheism* (Philadelphia: Fortress, 1988; 2d ed; Edinburgh: T & T Clark, 1998), esp. 99–124.

8. "Son of God" (e.g., Acts 9:20; Rom 1:4; John 3:18) and references to "his" (God's) Son (e.g., 1 Thess 1:10; Rom 8:32); "Image of God" (2 Cor 4:4; Col 1:15); "Lamb of God" (John 1:36); God's "Servant" (Acts 4:27, 30); God's "Messiah" (e.g., Acts 3:18); "Word" (John 1:1-3, 14); "the Son" (Matt 11:27/Luke 10:22).

9. For a robust and extended analysis of NT passages where *theos* may be applied to Jesus, see Murray J. Harris, *Jesus as God: The New Testament Use of Theos in Reference to Jesus* (Grand Rapids: Baker Book House, 1992).

10. I have given a much fuller discussion of the presentation of Jesus in GJohn in *Lord Jesus Christ: Devotion to Jesus in Earliest Christianity* (Grand Rapids: Eerdmans, 2003), 349–407.

11. Marianne Meye Thompson, *The God of the Gospel of John* (Grand Rapids: Eerdmans, 2001).

12. Paul N. Anderson, *The Christology of the Fourth Gospel* (WUNT 2/78; Tübingen: Mohr-Siebeck, 1996).

13. These are examples of what is sometimes called the "divine passive," passive verbs with an unspecified subject of the verb but obviously referring to God's actions, e.g., Mark 3:28, "will be forgiven (by God)"; Mark 16:6, "he has been raised (by God)."

14. "He who did not withhold [*ouk epheisato*] his own son [*tou idiou huiou*]" in Romans 8:32 seems to echo Genesis 22:16, God's commendation of Abraham, "You did not withhold [*ouk epheisō*] your beloved son [*tou huiou sou tou agapētou*]."

15. Ernst Käsemann's claim that Jesus' obedience in Phil 2:7-8 is to cosmic spiritual forces has rightly been judged exegesis driven by Käsemann's positing of a gnostic redeemer myth behind the Philippians passage. Cf. Ernst Käsemann, "A Critical Analysis of Philippians 2:5-11," in *God and Christ: Existence and Province* (ed. R. W. Funk; New York: Harper, 1968), 45–88; Larry W. Hurtado, "Jesus as Lordly Example in Philippians 2:5-11," in *From Jesus to Paul: Studies in Honour of Francis Wright Beare* (ed. P. Richardson and J. C. Hurd; Waterloo: Wilfrid Laurier University Press, 1984), 113–26.

16. I suggest that Christian beliefs about Jesus' own divine "nature" should be framed to do justice to the clear NT presentation of Jesus as recipient of divine vindication.

17. This "finger of God" phrase likely derives from (and may allude to) the biblical account of the contest between Aaron and the magicians of Egypt (Exod 8:19).

18. I take John 14:13-14 ("Whatever you ask in my name, I will do it, that the Father may be glorified in the Son") as meaning that, as God's unique "Son," Jesus will respond to petitions addressed to "the Father" in Jesus' name.

19. We are apparently to think that John supposed the angel to be God. See the major study of the topos of angelic refusal of worship that one finds in a number of ancient Jewish texts and reflected also in Revelation: Loren T. Stuckenbruck, *Angel Veneration and Christology* (WUNT 2/70; Tübingen: Mohr-Siebeck, 1995).

20. Richard J. Bauckham, "The Worship of Jesus in Apocalyptic Christianity," *NTS* 27 (1981): 322–41.

21. Larry W. Hurtado, "The Binitarian Shape of Early Christian Worship," in *The Jewish Roots of Christological Monotheism: Papers from the St. Andrews Conference on the Historical Origins of the Worship of Jesus* (ed. Carey C. Newman, James R. Davilia, and Gladys S. Lewis; Leiden: Brill, 1999), 187–213, which appears as chapter three of L. W. Hurtado, *At the Origins of Christian Worship* (Carlisle, England: Paternoster, 1999; Grand Rapids: Eerdmans, 2000); and idem, *How on Earth Did Jesus Become a God? Historical Questions about Earliest Devotion to Jesus* (Grand Rapids: Eerdmans, 2005), 48–53.

22. Richard J. Bauckham, "The Worship of Jesus," in *The Climax of Prophecy: Studies on the Book of Revelation* (Edinburgh: T & T Clark, 1993), 118–49; idem, "Jesus, Worship of," in *ABD*, 3:812–19.

23. Larry W. Hurtado, "Lord," in *DPL*, 560–69.

24. On the formulae that characterize the openings and closings of Paul's letters, and possible connections with liturgical usage, see J. L. Wu, "Liturgical Elements," *DPL*, 557–60; Peter T. O'Brien, *Introductory Thanksgivings in the Letters of Paul* (NovTSup 49; Leiden: E. J. Brill, 1977); Jeffrey A. D. Weima, *Neglected Endings: The Significance of the Pauline Letter Closings* (JSNTSup 101; Sheffield: JSOT Press, 1994).

25. Larry J. Kreitzer, *Jesus and God in Paul's Eschatology* (JSNTSup 19; Sheffield: JSOT Press, 1987); Carl J. Davis, *The Name and Way of the Lord* (JSNTSup 129; Sheffield: JSOT Press, 1996).

26. C. F. D. Moule, *Worship in the New Testament* (Bramcote: Grove Books, 1983), 66. I do not engage here the disputed issue of whether *maranatha* derives from a specifically eucharistic setting. Cf., e.g., Raymond F. Collins, *First Corinthians* (SP; Collegeville: Liturgical Press, 1999), 614–15; Anthony C. Thiselton, *The First Epistle to the Corinthians* (NIGTC; Grand Rapids: Eerdmans, 2000), 1348–52.

27. I have discussed the phenomena and texts referring to "Wisdom" and "Logos" more fully in *One God, One Lord*, 41–50.

28. The ancient Jewish encounter with Greek philosophical currents in the Hellenistic period likely helped shape the sort of grand claims for Torah that we have in Sirach and Baruch, Torah thus defined as the ultimate philosophy and way of life.

29. E.g., Eldon Jay Epp, "Wisdom, Torah, Word: The Johannine Prologue and the Purpose of the Fourth Gospel," in *Current Issues in Biblical and Patristic Interpretation: Studies in Honor of M. C. Tenney* (ed. G. F. Hawthorne; Grand Rapids: Eerdmans, 1971), 128–46. But cf. J. E. Fossum, "In the Beginning Was the Name: Onomanology as the Key to Johannine Christology," in *The Image of the Invisible God: Essays on the Influence of Jewish Mysticism on Early Christology* (Freiburg/Göttingen: Universitätsverlag Freiburg/Vandenhoeck & Ruprecht, 1995), 109–34, who contends that traditions of God's name also played a role in John's Christology.

30. On Col 1:15-20, see now especially Christian Stettler, *Der Kolosserhymnus: Untersuchungen zu Form, traditionsgeschichtlichem Hintergrund und Aussage von Kol 1,15-20* (WUNT 2/131; Tübingen: Mohr-Siebeck, 2000). On the use of Wisdom traditions in the NT more broadly, see, e.g., Elisabeth Schüssler Fiorenza, "Wisdom Mythology and the Christological Hymns of the New Testament," in *Aspects of Wisdom in Judaism and Early Christianity* (ed. R. L. Wilken; Notre Dame: University of Notre Dame Press, 1975), 17–41.

31. I discuss these and other texts pertaining to this matter in *One God, One Lord*, 51–69.

32. Larry W. Hurtado, "Pre-Existence," in *DPL*, 743–46.

33. Cf., e.g., J. D. G. Dunn, "Let John Be John: A Gospel for Its Time," in *The Gospel and the Gospels* (ed. Peter Stuhlmacher; Grand Rapids: Eerdmans, 1991), 293–322. After reading an earlier draft of this chapter, Dunn insisted to me that he does not mean to represent the connection of Jesus and divine Wisdom as "no more than inspiration" and that he does intend in some sense "incarnation." But it still seems to me that his heavy emphasis on divine Wisdom acts too much as a controlling category in his interpretation of NT statements about Jesus' "preexistence." Indeed, I do not think that biblical/Jewish Wisdom traditions were as central for Paul as Dunn supposes. In any case, wherever Jewish/OT Wisdom traditions are appropriated, I take the NT as (re)defining divine Wisdom in light of Jesus. The major study is Hermann von Lips, *Weisheitliche Traditionen im Neuen Testament* (WMANT 64; Neukirchen-Vluyn: Neukirchener Verlag, 1990).

34. See, e.g., E. E. Ellis, *Paul's Use of the Old Testament* (1957; reprint, Grand Rapids: Baker Book House, 1981), 67; and now the review of issues in Thiselton, *First Epistle to the Corinthians*, 727–30.

35. There are three variants in the Greek manuscripts of 1 Corinthians 10:9: "Christ" ($\mathfrak{P}^{46}$, D, et al.), "the Lord" (א, B, et al.), and "God" (A, et al.). Taking account of the respective antiquity and generally perceived value of the textual witnesses in question and also the likely nature of deliberate scribal changes, it seems probable that either "Christ" or "the Lord" was the original reading. In either case, Jesus was the referent.

36. In John 17:5, Jesus asks, "Father, glorify me in your own presence with the glory that I had in your presence before the world existed," which makes it possible that in 12:41 the author means that Isaiah saw the preincarnate Son. Other early Christian texts, however (e.g., *Ascension of Isaiah*), posit that Isaiah saw God and identify the Son as one of the Seraphim. See Darrell D. Hannah, "Isaiah's Vision in the Ascension of Isaiah and the Early Church," *JTS* 50 (1999): 80–101.

37. Nils A. Dahl, "Christ, Creation and the Church," in *The Background of the New Testament and Its Eschatology: Studies in Honour of C. H. Dodd* (ed. W. D. Davies and D. Daube; Cambridge: Cambridge University Press, 1954), 422–43; reprinted in N. A. Dahl, *Jesus in the Memory of the Early Church* (Minneapolis: Augsburg, 1976), 120–40.

38. In Rev 13:8 "from the foundation of the world" could also be understood as referring to the slaying of the Lamb, but in 17:8 the phrase rather more clearly refers to the writing of the names of the elect.

39. Dahl, "Christ, Creation and Church."

40. Hurtado, *One God, One Lord*, 93–128; *How on Earth Did Jesus Become a God?* 25–30.

4. The Spirit and "God" in the New Testament

1. Key studies include earlier works by Hermann Gunkel, *The Influence of the Holy Spirit: The Popular View of the Apostolic Age and the Teaching of the Apostle Paul* (Philadelphia: Fortress, 1979 [German 1888]); Henry Barclay Swete, *The Holy Spirit in the New Testament* (London: Macmillan, 1909); Ernest F. Scott, *The Spirit in the New Testament* (London: Hodder and Stoughton, 1923); Friedrich Büchsel, *Der Geist Gottes im Neuen Testament* (Gütersloh: C. Bertelsmann, 1926); and more recent important studies by J. D. G. Dunn, *Jesus and the Spirit: A Study of the Religious and Charismatic Experience of Jesus and the First Christians as Reflected in the New Testament* (London: SCM, 1975); Robert P. Menzies, *The Development of Early Christian Pneumatology with Special Reference to Luke-Acts* (JSNTSup 54; Sheffield: Sheffield Academic Press, 1991); Max-Alain Chevalier, *Souffle de Dieu: Le Saint-Esprit dans le Nouveau Testament* (3 vols; Paris: Beauchesne, 1978–91); Gordon D. Fee, *God's Empowering Presence: The Holy Spirit in the Letters of Paul* (Peabody, Mass.: Hendrickson, 1994); and now John R. Levison, *Filled with the Spirit* (Grand Rapids: Eerdmans, 2009).

2. In this chapter, for the sake of economy of words, I shall often refer to the divine Spirit simply as "the Spirit."

3. I draw here on Jacob Kremer, "πνεῦμα," *EDNT*, 3:118. See also, Eberhard Kamlah et al., "Spirit," *NIDNTT*, 3:689–709, esp. 693–706 on the Spirit in the NT.

4. See, e.g., the review of "Spirit in the OT" by Friedrich Baumgärtel, "πνευμα," *TDNT*, 6:359–67; and more fully R. Albertz and Claus Westermann, "רוח *ruah* spirit," *TLOT*, 3:1202–20 (esp. 1212–20); H.-J. Fabry, "רוח," *ThWAT*, 7:386–426; M. V. Van Pelt et al., "רוח," *NIDOTTE*, 3:1073–78; Büchsel, *Der Geist Gottes*, 1–36; Chevalier, *Souffle de Dieu*, 1:19–35.

5. There are a few additional instances of "holy Spirit" in the Greek OT: e.g., Dan 5:12; 6:4 (LXX, *pneuma hagion*); Wis 9:17 (*to hagion sou pneuma*).

6. Erik Sjöberg, "πνευμα," *TDNT*, 6:381.

7. "All flesh" could even be taken to mean a dispensing of the Spirit beyond the people of Israel. Cf. the oracle in Ezek 39:29 promising "I [will] pour out my Spirit upon the house of Israel, says the Lord GOD." Similar oracles of a future bestowal of divine Spirit include Ezek 36:27; 37:14; Isa 32:15; 44:3.

8. See, e.g., Menzies, *Development of Early Christian Pneumatology*, 52–112. John R. Levison, *The Spirit in First-Century Judaism* (AGJU 29; Leiden: Brill, 1997) offers an in-depth study of "spirit" in Josephus, Philo, and Pseudo-Philo; Levison, *Filled with the Spirit*, 109–217, for a broader review of Second Temple Jewish texts. Chevalier, *Souffle de Dieu*, 1:44–73; and (of an earlier vintage) Büchsel, *Der Geist Gottes*, 54–99.

9. Levison, *Spirit in First-Century Judaism*, 244, 246.

10. Ibid., 248.

11. Menzies, *Development of Early Christian Pneumatology*, e.g., 112.

12. Ibid., 89. There are several Qumran manuscripts that witness to the Hymns, among which 1QHᵃ is the most substantially preserved. My references are to the translation and numbering of columns and lines in Florentino García Martínez, *The Dead Sea Scrolls Translated: The Qumran Texts in English* (2d ed.; Grand Rapids: Eerdmans, 1996).

13. Arthur Everett Sekki, *The Meaning of Ruah at Qumran* (SBLDS 110; Atlanta: Scholars, 1989), 82–83.

14. I cite the translation of these lines in García Martínez, *Dead Sea Scrolls Translated*, 343.

15. E.g., the LXX is about three times the size of the Greek NT.

16. Sekki, *Meaning of Ruah at Qumran*, 71.

17. John J. Collins and Robert A. Kugler, eds., *Religion in the Dead Sea Scrolls* (Grand Rapids: Eerdmans, 2000); David E. Aune, *The Cultic Setting of Realized Eschatology in Early Christianity* (NovTSup 28; Leiden: E. J. Brill, 1972) discussed how corporate worship in Qumran and earliest Christianity was regarded as the setting for experience of eschatological realities.

18. See, e.g., the discussion in Fee, *God's Empowering Presence*, 121–27.

19. See, e.g., the survey of references/uses in Kamlah et al., "Spirit," *NIDNTT*, 3:693–95.

20. Figures can be only approximate as exegetes will differ in a few instances as to whether *pneuma* designates the divine/Holy Spirit (e.g., John 4:23-24; 6:63).

21. Swete, *Holy Spirit in the New Testament*, 287–88.

22. J. D. G. Dunn, *The Theology of Paul the Apostle* (Grand Rapids: Eerdmans, 1998), 417.

23. E.g., F. Hahn, "χριστος," *EDNT*, 3:478–86.

24. Swete, *Holy Spirit in the New Testament*, 352–60.

25. See, e.g., C. E. B. Cranfield, *The Epistle to the Romans, Volume 1* (ICC; Edinburgh: T & T Clark, 1975), 417–18; A. Sand, "απαρχη," *EDNT*, 1:116–17.

26. E.g., A. Sand, "αρραβων," *EDNT*, 1:157–58.

27. Harold W. Attridge, *The Epistle to the Hebrews* (Hermeneia; Philadelphia: Fortress, 1989), 170.

28. See esp. James D. G. Dunn, *New Testament Theology: An Introduction* (Nashville: Abingdon Press, 2009), 32–37; idem, *Jesus and the Spirit*, for a wide-ranging discussion of NT texts. On Paul in particular, see Dunn, *Theology of Paul*, 426–34, and Fee, *God's Empowering Presence*.

29. E.g., G. W. H. Lampe, "The Holy Spirit in the Writings of St. Luke," in *Studies in the Gospels: Essays in Memory of R. H. Lightfoot* (ed. Dennis E. Nineham; Oxford: Basil Blackwell, 1967), 159–200; Menzies, *Development of Early Christian Pneumatology*.

30. Dunn judged Romans 8:1-27 as "unquestionably the high point of Paul's theology of the Spirit" (*Theology of Paul*, 423).

31. Max Turner, "The Spirit of Christ and Christology," in *Christ the Lord: Studies Presented to Donald Guthrie* (ed. H. H. Rowdon; Leicester: InterVarsity, 1982), 168–90; idem, "The Spirit of Christ and 'Divine' Christology," in *Jesus of Nazareth, Lord and Christ* (ed. Joel B. Green and Max Turner; Grand Rapids: Eerdmans, 1994), 413–36. In the latter, he conducts a critical dialogue with views of J. D. G. Dunn as laid out esp. in *Christology in the Making* (London: SCM, 1980), 136–49. The fullest treatment of Pauline evidence is in Mehrdad Fatehi, *The Spirit's Relation to the Risen Lord in Paul* (WUNT 2/128; Tübingen: Mohr Siebeck, 2000). Gordon D. Fee makes much of the Spirit-Jesus connection as well in Paul's writings: *Pauline Christology* (Peabody, Mass.: Hendrickson, 2007), 586–93. I cite here from Fatehi's characterization of Pauline data (303), which is also applicable more broadly across NT texts. Both Turner and Fatehi also refer to " 'divine' christology" (e.g., Fatehi, *Spirit's Relation*, 311–30).

32. Swete, *Holy Spirit in the New Testament*, 278.

33. As noted by G. K. Beale, "in the Spirit" in 1:10 "uses the language of the prophet Ezekiel's repeated rapture in the Spirit, thus giving John's revelation prophetic authority like that of the OT prophets (cf. Ezek 2:2; 3:12, 14, 24; 11:1; 43:5)," *The Book of Revelation* (NIGTC; Grand Rapids: Eerdmans, 1999), 203.

34. Turner, " 'Divine' Christology," 423.

35. On the likely import of Jesus' breathing upon his disciples here as an allusion to God's breath in the creation of life (Gen 1:7; Wis 15:11), see, e.g., R. E. Brown, *The Gospel According to John, XIII-XXI* (Garden City, N.Y.: Doubleday, 1970), 1037.

36. In 𝔓⁴⁶, "his Son" (*tou huiou*) is absent, so the statement reads "God sent forth his Spirit into our hearts." This could represent an accidental omission, arising from the similarity of final letters in *huiou* and *autou* ("his"), or a deliberate omission, perhaps prompted by the unusual expression "the Spirit of his Son." It is less likely that the words were added, as the resulting expression is unique in the NT. So also Philip W. Comfort, *New Testament Text and Translation Commentary* (Carol Stream, Ill.: Tyndale House, 2008), 566–67.

37. See, e.g., H. D. Betz, *Galatians* (Hermeneia Commentaries; Philadelphia: Fortress, 1979), 210.

38. For discussion, see, e.g., Fee, *God's Empowering Presence*, 742–43; G. F. Hawthorne, *Philippians* (WBC; Waco: Word Books, 1983), 40–41.

39. In the copying of Acts, there were various efforts to modify this unique expression, "the Spirit of Jesus," replacing it with more familiar phrases, e.g., "the Spirit of the Lord" or "the Holy Spirit." But the difficulty of the expression speaks in favor of it being original, and moreover, the supporting manuscripts are strong. See Bruce M. Metzger, *A Textual Commentary on the Greek New Testament* (2d ed.; London/New York: United Bible Societies, 1994), 390–91.

40. This has been the majority view among modern exegetes, e.g., Swete, *Holy Spirit in the New Testament*, 192–96; Chevalier, *Souffle de Dieu*, 2:292–95; Paul Barnett, *The Second Epistle to the Corinthians* (NICNT; Grand Rapids: Eerdmans, 1997), 196–99; David B. Capes, *Old Testament Yahweh Texts in Paul's Christology* (WUNT 2/47; Tübingen: Mohr

Siebeck, 1992), 155–57; and esp. Fatehi, *Spirit's Relation*, 289–302. For the view that *Kyrios* in 3:17 is not a reference to Jesus, however, cf., e.g., Margaret E. Thrall, *The Second Epistle to the Corinthians* (vol. 1; ICC; Edinburgh, 1994), 266–90 (esp. 271–73); J. D. G. Dunn, "2 Corinthians III.17—'The Lord Is the Spirit'," *JTS* 21 (1970): 309–20; idem, *Theology of Paul the Apostle* , 421–22; and Fee, *God's Empowering Presence*, 309–20. Thrall takes 3:16-17 as Paul advocating "a conversion to the Spirit" (274), and Dunn uses somewhat similar language ("2 Corinthians III.17," 313; *Theology*, 422), but it is not quite clear what this could be. In this view, the passage has little to do specifically with the relation of the Spirit and Jesus, which I find dubious. On Paul's use of *Kyrios* see L. W. Hurtado, "Lord," *DPL*, 560–69.

41. Ingo Hermann, *Kyrios und Pneuma: Studien zur Christologi der Paulinischen Hauptbriefe* (SUNT 2; Munich: Kösel-Verlag, 1961), 38, rightly noted that 3:16 is a rather free adaptation of Exod 34:34, Paul producing thereby a genuinely new statement of christological import.

42. Cf. Dunn, "2 Corinthians III.17," 317–18, who insists that in 3:17 "the Lord" is *Yahweh* and contends that "the central antithesis" in 2 Cor 3 is "between the law and the Spirit, not between the law and Christ" (318). But Dunn overlooks too much in making this statement. The new covenant (3:6) "of the Spirit" and of which Paul is minister is wholly to do with Jesus and his redemptive work. Moreover, for Paul, Israel's blindness and hardness of heart here (3:14-15) and elsewhere (Rom 11:25-29) amount to a refusal to recognize Jesus as Christ and Lord. Certainly, in the larger context (3:1–4:15), it is clear that Paul's concern is that people perceive "the gospel of the glory of Christ" (4:4) and "the knowledge of the glory of God in the face of Jesus Christ" (4:6).

43. For analysis of Paul's association of Jesus with divine "glory," see Carey C. Newman, *Paul's Glory-Christology: Tradition and Rhetoric* (NovTSup 69; Leiden: Brill, 1992).

44. Fatehi, *Spirit's Relation*, 304–5.

45. On 1 Cor 15:45, see, e.g., Fee, *God's Empowering Presence*, 264–67; Raymond F. Collins, *First Corinthians* (SP 7; Collegeville, Minn.: Liturgical, 1999), 568–72; Anthony C. Thiselton, *The First Epistle to the Corinthians* (NIGTC; Grand Rapids: Eerdmans, 2000), 1281–85. Cf. J. D. G. Dunn, "1 Corinthians 15:45—Last Adam, Life-giving Spirit," in *Christ and the Spirit in the New Testament* (ed. Barnabas Lindars and Stephen S. Smalley; Cambridge: Cambridge University Press, 1973), 127–41. Dunn rightly emphasizes that, in Paul's thought, believers experience the Spirit (of "God") through faith in Jesus, and so there is for Paul a close connection of Jesus and the Spirit. But he may overstretch things a bit in taking "became" (*egeneto*) in 15:45 as meaning that "in the believers' experience there is *no* distinction between Christ and Spirit" (139).

46. I draw here upon Turner's discussion of the matter in " 'Divine' Christology," 433.

5. Concluding Observations

1. Marianne Meye Thompson, *The Promise of the Father: Jesus and God in the New Testament* (Louisville: Westminster John Knox, 2000), esp. chs. 3–6; Christiane Zimmermann, *Die Namen des Vaters: Studien zu ausgewälten neutestamentlichen Gottesbezeichnungen vor ihrem frühjüdischen und paganen Sprachhorizont* (AJEC 69; Leiden: E. J. Brill, 2007), esp. 74–166.

2. Curiously, I can find no book-length scholarly study of "God" in GMatthew in English, German, or French.

3. For further discussion, see Richard Bauckham, *The Climax of Prophecy* (Edinburgh: T & T Clark, 1993), 118–49.

4. Michael A. Williams, *Rethinking "Gnosticism": An Argument for Dismantling a Dubious Category* (Princeton: Princeton University Press, 1996), 51–53.

5. Cf. James D. G. Dunn, *New Testament Theology: An Introduction* (Nashville: Abingdon Press, 2009), 7–9 (the phrase is from p. 9).

6. The term *triadic* is used in A. W. Wainwright, *The Trinity in the New Testament* (London: SPCK, 1962, 1969), 248, who refers to a "threefold pattern of thought about God" and "a triadic conception of God" reflected in the NT. Similarly, Gordon Fee, *Pauline Christology* (Peabody, Mass.: Hendrickson, 2007), refers to "Paul and the Divine Triad" (591).

7. Maurice Casey, *From Jewish Prophet to Gentile God: The Origins and Development of New Testament Christology* (Louisville: Westminster/John Knox; Cambridge: James Clarke and Co., 1991). "Fully" and "genuinely" divine here are my attempts to refer to the question of whether Jesus was treated as "divine" in the way that "God" is and not simply as a heavenly being such as a principal angel.

8. See, e.g., Dunn's discussion of the Pauline evidence in *The Theology of Paul the Apostle* (Grand Rapids: Eerdmans, 1998), 252–60. Dunn gives his critique of Casey in "The Making of Christology—Evolution or Unfolding?" in *Jesus of Nazareth, Lord and Christ* (ed. Joel B. Green and Max Turner; Grand Rapids: Eerdmans, 1994), 437–52.

9. E.g., Hurtado, *Lord Jesus Christ: Devotion to Jesus in Earliest Christianity* (Grand Rapids: Eerdmans, 2003), 134–53; idem, *How on Earth Did Jesus Become a God? Historical Questions about Earliest Devotion to Jesus* (Grand Rapids: Eerdmans, 2005), 31–55.

10. Richard Bauckham has proposed that the NT reflects an inclusion of Jesus in the "identity" of God, in *God Crucified: Monotheism and Christology in the New Testament* (Carlisle, England: Paternoster, 1998). His term rightly points to the extraordinarily close connection of Jesus with "God." But I think that Bauckham does not fully succeed in his claim that the representation of Jesus as sharing in creation and divine rule is unique or in his contention that this sort of conceptual link of Jesus with "God" is more significant than the devotional practice of earliest Christians in constituting a momentous religious development.

11. In Justin Martyr we have perhaps the earliest extant efforts to articulate the relationships of "God" and Jesus in terms and categories adapted from Greek philosophical traditions. Theophilus of Antioch (*Autol.* 2.15) gives the first use of the Greek word *trias* (triad), and Tertullian was first to use the Latin *trinitas* (*Prax.* 3) to capture the threeness of "God." For a summary of Patristic-era development of the doctrine of the Trinity, see David F. Wright, "Trinity," *EEC*, 1142–47 (with further references). Eric Osborn, *The Emergence of Christian Theology* (Cambridge: Cambridge University Press, 1993) focused on second-century developments, esp. 1–38, 173–96. I must dissent, however, from his somewhat simplistic and anachronistic view of the relationship between Christian doctrine and liturgical practice (e.g., 180–81).

12. Among possible examples of this in ancient settings, there is the recently discovered Christian mosaic from Megiddo, which has a dedication of a eucharistic table, which can be read as "to God, Jesus Christ, as a memorial." On the find, see Yotam Tepper and Leah Di Segni, *A Christian Prayer Hall of the Third Century CE at Kefar 'Othnay (Legio)* (Jerusalem: Israel Antiquities Authority, 2006).

13. The Synoptic Gospels refer to the Spirit driving (Mark 1:12) or leading (Matt 4:1; Luke 4:1) Jesus into the wilderness where he was tempted. But I do not regard these as constituting an exception.

14. Fee, *Pauline Christology*, 591. Key passages cited by Fee here and in other contexts include 2 Cor 13:13; 1 Cor 12:4-6; Eph 4:4-6.

15. I borrow the term *triangular* from J. D. G. Dunn's reference to the "triangular relationship" in which early Christians saw themselves, "in the Spirit, in sonship to the Father, in service to the Lord" (*Jesus and the Spirit* [Philadelphia: Westminster, 1975], 326).

16. See, e.g., Larry W. Hurtado, "'Jesus' as God's Name, and Jesus as God's Embodied Name in Justin Martyr," in *Justin Martyr and His Worlds* (ed. Sara Parvis and Paul Foster; Minneapolis: Fortress, 2007), 128–36.

17. The possible influence upon Christian thinking about the Trinity from Roman political theory has not, to my knowledge, been explored very much. On early Roman ideas of how the imperial office could accommodate more than one figure, see Ernst Kornemann, *Doppelprinzipat und Reichsteilung im Imperium Romanum* (Leipzig/Berlin: B. G. Teubner, 1930). Osborn, *Emergence*, emphasized the various intellectual forces helping to shape Christian doctrinal development in the second century.

18. The concluding chapter in Fee, *Pauline Christology*, 586–93, is entitled "Christ and the Spirit: Paul as a Proto-Trinitarian."

19. Fee, *God's Empowering Presence: The Holy Spirit in the Letters of Paul* (Peabody, Mass.: Hendrickson, 1994), 827.

20. Ibid., 839.

21. Ibid., 840.

22. Ibid., 838.

23. Ibid., 839, 841. The Pauline passages Fee cites as reflecting this "soteriological Trinitarianism" are 1 Thess 1:4-5; 2 Thess 2:13; 1 Cor 1:4-7; 2:4-5, 12; 6:11, 19-20; 2 Cor 1:21-22; Gal 3:1-5; Rom 8:3-4, 15-17; Col 3:16; Eph 1:17; 2:18, 20-22; Phil 3:3.

24. Wainwright, *Trinity in the New Testament*, 4 (emphasis mine).

25. Ibid., 3.

26. Ibid., 5.

27. Ibid., 7.

28. E.g., Larry W. Hurtado, *One God, One Lord: Early Christian Devotion and Ancient Jewish Monotheism* (Philadelphia: Fortress, 1988; 2d ed. Edinburgh: T & T Clark, 1998), 100–114; idem, *Lord Jesus Christ*, 134–53; idem, *How on Earth Did Jesus Become a God?* 48–53.

29. Wainwright, *Trinity in the New Testament*, 53.

30. Cf. Adela Yarbro Collins, "The Worship of Jesus and the Imperial Cult," in *The Jewish Roots of Christological Monotheism* (ed. Carey C. Newman, James R. Davila, and Gladys S. Lewis; JSJSup 63; Leiden: Brill, 1999), 234–57, who proposes that early believers were influenced toward treating Jesus as divine, whether consciously or unconsciously, in a significant measure by patterns of ruler-cult and related phenomena. It should be a salutary warning, however, that in his study of the question Stephan Lösch mounted a very strong case against the sort of view that Collins espouses: *Deitas Jesu und antike Apotheose: Ein Beitrag zur Exegese und Religionsgeschichte* (Rottenburg: Bader'sche Verlagsbuchhandlung, 1933). I have offered my own more modest statement on the matter in *How on Earth Did Jesus Become a God?* 31–55, esp.38–42.

31. Wainwright, *Trinity in the New Testament*, 88. According to Gal 1:15-19, Paul may have spent as much as three years in Damascus and Arabia.

32. Wilhelm Bousset, *Kyrios Christos* (trans. J. E. Steely; Nashville: Abingdon Press, 1970 [German 1913]), e.g., 153–55.

33. On Paul's early years, see Martin Hengel and Anna Maria Schwemer, *Paul Between Damascus and Antioch: The Unknown Years* (trans. John Bowden; London: SCM Press, 1997). On the earliest evidence of Jesus devotion, see Hurtado, *Lord Jesus Christ*, esp. 79–216.

34. I have laid out the argument presented here in earlier publications: e.g., *Lord Jesus Christ*, 175–76; *How on Earth Did Jesus Become a God?* 33–36.

35. Cf., e.g., discussion of Paul's statements in Gal 1:3-16 in Franz Mussner, *Der Galaterbrief* (3d ed.; Freiburg: Herder, 1977), 78–93; J. D. G. Dunn, *The Epistle to the Galatians* (London: A&C Black, 1993), 55–68.

36. Hurtado, *How on Earth Did Jesus Become a God?* 152–78, a republished version of my article "Pre-70 CE Jewish Opposition to Christ-Devotion," *JTS* 50 (1999): 35–58.

37. The key references to this conflict and the expulsion of Johannine believers from the larger Jewish community are John 9:22; 12:42; 16:1-3. For many scholars, the influential study is J. L. Martyn, *History and Theology in the Fourth Gospel* (rev. ed; Nashville: Abingdon Press, 1979 [1967]).

38. In 20:31, there are variant readings attested among manuscripts: "*pisteusēte*" (aorist: which could mean "that you may [come to] believe"), and "*pisteuēte*" (present: which could mean "that you may [continue to] believe").

39. In an earlier publication, I have offered a case for seeing GJohn as a programmatic presentation of the historic figure of Jesus with the cognitive benefit of the revelatory work of the Spirit-Paraclete: "Remembering and Revelation: The Historic and Glorified Jesus in the Gospel of John," in *Israel's God and Rebecca's Children* (ed. David B. Capes et al.; Waco: Baylor University Press, 2007), 195–213.

40. The only study devoted to this that I know is Adolf von Harnack, *Der Vorwurf des Atheismus in den drei ersten Jahrhunderten* (TU 13/1; Leipzig: J. C. Heinrichs, 1905). Cf. also Anders Bjorn Drachman, *Atheism in Pagan Antiquity* (London: Gyldenhal, 1922).

41. I suppose that the possible exceptions might arguably be Paul's Epistle to the Romans and the Epistle to the Hebrews.

BIBLIOGRAPHY

Albertz, R., and Claus Westermann. "רוּחַ *ruah* spirit." Pages 1202–20 in vol. 3 of *Theological Lexicon of the Old Testament*. Edited by Ernst Jenni and Claus Westermann. Translated by M. E. Biddle. 3 vols. Peabody, Mass.: Hendrickson, 1997.

Anderson, Paul N. *The Christology of the Fourth Gospel*. Wissenschaftliche Untersuchungen zum Neuen Testament. Reihe 2/78. Tübingen: Mohr Siebeck, 1996.

———. "The Having-Sent-Me Father: Aspects of Agency, Encounter, and Irony in the Johannine Father-Son Relationship." *Semeia* 85 (1999): 33–57.

Athanassiadi, Polymnia, and Michael Frede, eds. *Pagan Monotheism in Late Antiquity*. Oxford: Clarendon, 1999.

Attridge, Harold W. *The Epistle to the Hebrews*. Hermeneia. Philadelphia: Fortress, 1989.

Aune, David E. *The Cultic Setting of Realized Eschatology in Early Christianity*. Supplements to Novum Testamentum 28. Leiden: E. J. Brill, 1972.

Bahr, Gordon J. "The Use of the Lord's Prayer in the Primitive Church." *Journal of Biblical Literature* 84 (1965): 153–59. Repr. pages 149–55 in *The Lord's Prayer and Jewish Liturgy*. New York: Seabury, 1978.

Balz, Horst, and Gerhard Schneider, eds. *Exegetical Dictionary of the New Testament*. Translated by James W. Thompson and John W. Medendorp. 3 vols. Grand Rapids: Eerdmans, 1990–1993.

Barnett, Paul. *The Second Epistle to the Corinthians*. New International Commentary on the New Testament. Grand Rapids: Eerdmans, 1997.

Barrett, C. K. "Christocentric or Theocentric? Observations on the Theological Method of the Fourth Gospel." Pages 1–18 in *Essays on John*. London: SPCK, 1982.

———. " 'The Father is greater than I' (John 14.28): Subordinationist Christology in the New Testament." Pages 19–36 in *Essays on John*. Philadelphia: Westminster, 1982.

Bassler, Jouette. "God in the NT." Pages 1049–55 in vol. 2 of *Anchor Bible Dictionary*. Edited by D. N. Freedman. 6 vols. New York: Doubleday, 1992.

Bauckham, Richard J. *The Climax of Prophecy*. Edinburgh: T & T Clark, 1993.

———. "Jesus, Worship of." Pages 812–19 in vol. 3 of *Anchor Bible Dictionary*. Edited by D. N. Freedman. 6 vols. New York: Doubleday, 1992.

———. "The Worship of Jesus." Pages 118–49 in *The Climax of Prophecy: Studies on the Book of Revelation*. Edinburgh: T & T Clark, 1993.

———. "The Worship of Jesus in Apocalyptic Christianity." *New Testament Studies* 27 (1981): 322–41.

Baumgärtel, Friedrich. "πνευμα." Pages 359–67 in vol. 6 of *Theological Dictionary of the New Testament*. Edited by G. Kittel and G. Friedrich. Translated by G. W. Bromiley. 10 vols. Grand Rapids: Eerdmans, 1964–1976.

Beale, G. K. *The Book of Revelation*. New International Greek Testament Commentary. Grand Rapids: Eerdmans, 1999.

Beierwaltes, Werner. "The Love of Beauty and the Love of God." Pages 293–313 in *Classical Mediterranean Spirituality*. Edited by A. H. Armstrong. New York: Crossroad, 1986.

Betz, H. D. *Galatians*. Hermeneia. Philadelphia: Fortress, 1979.

Botterweck, G. J., and H. Ringgren, eds. *Theologisches Wörterbuch zum Alten Testament*. Stuttgart: Kohlhammer, 1970–.

Böttrich, Christfried. "Die neutestamentliche Rede von Gott im Spiegel der Gottesprädikationen." *Berliner Theologische Zeitschrift* 1 (1999): 59–80.

Bousset, Wilhelm. *Kyrios Christos: A History of the Belief in Christ from the Beginnings of Christianity to Irenaeus*. Translated by J. E. Steely. Nashville: Abingdon Press, 1970.

Bradshaw, Paul. "God, Christ, and the Holy Spirit in Early Christian Praying." Pages 51–64 in *The Place of Christ in Liturgical Prayer: Trinity, Christology, and Liturgical Theology*. Edited by Bryan D. Spinks. Collegeville, Minn.: Liturgical, 2008.

Brawley, Robert L. *Centering on God: Method and Message in Luke-Acts*. Louisville: Westminster John Knox, 1990.

Brown, Colin, ed. *New International Dictionary of New Testament Theology*. 4 vols. Grand Rapids: Zondervan, 1975–1985.

Brown, R. E. *The Gospel according to John, XIII-XXI*. Anchor Bible 29A. Garden City, N.Y.: Doubleday, 1970.

Büchsel, Friedrich. *Der Geist Gottes im Neuen Testament*. Gütersloh: C. Bertelsmann, 1926.

Capes, David B. *Old Testament Yahweh Texts in Paul's Christology*. Wissenschaftliche Untersuchungen zum Neuen Testament. Reihe 2/47. Tübingen: Mohr Siebeck, 1992.

Carroll, John T. "The God of Israel and the Salvation of the Nations." Pages 91–106 in *The Forgotten God: Perspectives in Biblical Theology*. Edited by A. Andrew Das and Frank J. Matera. Louisville: Westminster John Knox, 2002.

Casey, Maurice. *From Jewish Prophet to Gentile God: The Origins and Development of New Testament Christology*. Louisville: Westminster John Knox; Cambridge: James Clarke and Co., 1991.

Castelli, Elizabeth A. "Imperial Reimaginings of Christian Origins: Epic in Prudentius' Poem for the Martyr Eulalia." Pages 173–84 in *Reimagining Christian Origins: A Colloquium Honoring Burton L. Mack*. Edited by Elizabeth A. Castelli and Hal Taussig. Valley Forge, Pa.: Trinity Press International, 1996.

Chen, Diane G. *God as Father in Luke-Acts*. Studies in Biblical Literature 92. Bern/Frankfurt: Peter Lang, 2006.

Chevalier, Max-Alain. *Souffle de Dieu: Le Saint-Esprit dans le Nouveau Testament*. 3 vols. Paris: Beauchesne, 1978–91.

Collins, Adela Yarbro. "The Worship of Jesus and the Imperial Cult." Pages 234–57 in *The Jewish Roots of Christological Monotheism*. Edited by Carey C. Newman, James R. Davila, and Gladys S. Lewis. Supplements to the Journal for the Study of Judaism, vol. 63. Leiden: Brill, 1999.

Collins, John J., and Robert A. Kugler, eds. *Religion in the Dead Sea Scrolls*. Grand Rapids: Eerdmans, 2000.

Collins, Raymond F. *First Corinthians*. Sacra Pagina 7. Collegeville, Minn.: Liturgical, 1999.

Comfort, Philip W. *New Testament Text and Translation Commentary*. Carol Stream, Ill.: Tyndale House, 2008.

Cranfield, C. E. B. Romans 1–8. Volume 1 of *The Epistle to the Romans*. International Critical Commentary. Edinburgh: T & T Clark.

Cullmann, Oscar. *Christology of the New Testament*. Translated by Shirley C. Guthrie and Charles A. M. Hall. Philadelphia: Westminster, 1963.

Dahl, Nils Alstrup. "The Arrogant Archon and the Lewd Sophia: Jewish Traditions in Gnostic Revolt." Pages 689–712 in *Sethian Gnosticism*. Vol. 2 of *The Rediscovery of Gnosticism*. Edited by Bentley Layton. Leiden: E. J. Brill, 1981.

———. "Christ, Creation and the Church." Pages 422–43 in *The Background of the New Testament and Its Eschatology: Studies in Honour of C. H. Dodd*. Edited by W. D. Davies and D. Daube. Cambridge: Cambridge University Press, 1954. Repr. pages 120–40 in Nils Alstrup Dahl. *Jesus in the Memory of the Early Church*. Minneapolis: Augsburg, 1976.

———. "The Neglected Factor in New Testament Theology." *Reflections* 75 (1975): 5–8. Repr. pages 153–63 in *Jesus the Christ: The Historical Origins of Christological Doctrine*. Edited by Donald H. Juel. Minneapolis: Fortress, 1991.

Danove, Paul. "The Narrative Function of Mark's Characterization of God." *Novum Testamentum* 43 (2001): 12–30.

Das, A. Andrew, and Frank J. Matera, eds. *The Forgotten God: Perspectives in Biblical Theology*. Louisville: Westminster John Knox, 2002.

Davis, Carl J. *The Name and Way of the Lord*. Journal for the Study of the New Testament: Supplement Series 129. Sheffield: JSOT, 1996.

Donahue, John R. "A Neglected Factor in the Theology of Mark." *Journal of Biblical Literature* 101 (1982): 563–94.

Downing, F. Gerald. *God with Everything: The Divine in the Discourse of the First Christian Century*. Sheffield: Sheffield Phoenix, 2008.

Drachman, Anders Bjorn. *Atheism in Pagan Antiquity*. London: Gyldenhal, 1922.

Dunn, J. D. G. *Christology in the Making: A New Testament Inquiry into the Origins of the Doctrine of the Incarnation*. Philadelphia: Westminster, 1980. 2d ed. London: SCM, 1989.

———. *The Epistle to the Galatians*. London: A&C Black, 1993.

———. *Jesus and the Spirit: A Study of the Religious and Charismatic Experience of Jesus and the First Christians as Reflected in the New Testament*. London: SCM; Philadelphia: Fortress, 1975.

———. *New Testament Theology: An Introduction*. Nashville: Abingdon Press, 2009.

———. *The Theology of Paul the Apostle*. Edinburgh: T & T Clark; Grand Rapids: Eerdmans, 1998.

———. "2 Corinthians III.17—'The Lord is the Spirit'." *Journal of Theological Studies* 21 (1970): 309–20.

———. "Let John Be John: A Gospel for Its Time." Pages 293–322 in *The Gospel and the Gospels*. Edited by Peter Stuhlmacher. Grand Rapids: Eerdmans, 1991.

———. "The Making of Christology—Evolution or Unfolding?" Pages 437–52 in *Jesus of Nazareth, Lord and Christ*. Edited by Joel B. Green and Max Turner. Grand Rapids: Eerdmans, 1994.

Dunn, J. D. G., Colin Brown, and Eberhard Kamlah. "Spirit." Pages 693–95 in vol. 3 of *New International Dictionary of New Testament Theology*. Edited by Colin Brown. 4 vols. Grand Rapids: Zondervan, 1975–1985.

Edwards, Richard M. Review of Jerome H. Neyrey, *Render to God: New Testament Understandings of the Divine*. *RBL* 05/2005.

Ellis, E. E. *Paul's Use of the Old Testament*. Edinburgh: Oliver and Boyd, 1957. Repr., Grand Rapids: Baker Book House, 1981.

Epp, Eldon Jay. "Wisdom, Torah, Word: The Johannine Prologue and the Purpose of the Fourth Gospel." Pages 128–46 in *Current Issues in Biblical and Patristic Interpretation: Studies in Honor of M. C. Tenney*. Edited by G. F. Hawthorne. Grand Rapids: Eerdmans, 1971.

Fabry, Heinz-Josef. "רוח." Pages 386–426 in vol. 7 of *Theologisches Wörterbuch zum Alten Testament*. Edited by G. J. Botterweck and H. Ringgren. Stuttgart: Kohlhammer, 1970–.

Fatehi, Mehrdad. *The Spirit's Relation to the Risen Lord in Paul: An Examination of Its Christological Implications*. Wissenschaftliche Untersuchungen zum Neuen Testament. Reihe 2/128. Tübingen: Mohr Siebeck, 2000.

Fee, Gordon D. *The First Epistle to the Corinthians*. New International Commentary on the New Testament. Grand Rapids: Eerdmans, 1987.

———. *God's Empowering Presence: The Holy Spirit in the Letters of Paul*. Peabody, Mass.: Hendrickson, 1994.

———. *Pauline Christology: An Exegetical-Theological Study*. Peabody, Mass.: Hendrickson, 2007.

Ferguson, Everett, ed. *Encyclopedia of Early Christianity*. 2d ed. New York: Garland, 1990.

Fergusson, David. *Faith and Its Critics: A Conversation*. Oxford: Oxford University Press, 2009.

Fossum, J. E. "In the Beginning Was the Name: Onomanology As the Key to Johannine Christology." Pages 109–34 in *The Image of the Invisible God: Essays on the Influence of Jewish Mysticism on Early Christology*. Freiburg/Göttingen: Universitätsverlag Freiburg/Vandenhoeck & Ruprecht, 1995.

Freedman, D. N. *Anchor Bible Dictionary*. 6 vols. New York: Doubleday, 1992.

García Martínez, Florentino. *The Dead Sea Scrolls Translated: The Qumran Texts in English*. 2d ed. Grand Rapids: Eerdmans, 1996.

Gathercole, Simon J. "A Law unto Themselves: The Gentiles in Rom 2.14-15 Revisited." *Journal for the Study of the New Testament*, no. 85 (2000): 27–49.

Grant, Robert M. *The Gods and the One God*. Philadelphia: Westminster, 1986.

Green, J. B., S. McKnight, and I. H. Marshall, eds. *Dictionary of Jesus and the Gospels*. Downers Grove, Ill.: InterVarsity, 1992.

Gunkel, Hermann. *The Influence of the Holy Spirit: The Popular View of the Apostolic Age and the Teaching of the Apostle Paul*. Translated by Roy A. Harrisville and Philip A. Quanbeck II. Philadelphia: Fortress, 1979.

Guthrie, Donald, and R. P. Martin, "God." Pages 354–69 in *Dictionary of Paul and His Letters*. Edited by G. F. Hawthorne, R. P. Martin, and D. G. Reid. Downers Grove, Ill.: InterVarsity, 1993.

Guttenberger, Gudrun. *Die Gottesvorstellung im Markusevangelium.* Beihefte zur Zeitschrift für die neutestamentliche Wissenschaft 123. Berlin: Walter de Gruyter, 2004.

Hahn, F. "χριστος." Pages 478–86 in vol. 3 of *Exegetical Dictionary of the New Testament.* Edited by Horst Balz and Gerhard Schneider. Translated by James W. Thompson and John W. Medendorp. 3 vols. Grand Rapids: Eerdmans, 1990–1993.

Hannah, Darrell D. "Isaiah's Vision in the Ascension of Isaiah and the Early Church." *Journal of Theological Studies* 50, no. 1 (1999): 80–101.

Hanson, R. P. C. *The Search for the Christian Doctrine of God: The Arian Controversy.* Edinburgh: T & T Clark, 1988.

Harnack, Adolf von. *Der Vorwurf des Atheismus in den drei ersten Jahrhunderten.* Texte und Untersuchungen 13/1. Leipzig: J. C. Heinrichs, 1905.

Harris, Murray J. *Jesus As God: The New Testament Use of* Theos *in Reference to Jesus.* Grand Rapids: Baker Book House, 1992.

Hawthorne, G. F. *Philippians.* Word Biblical Commentary 43. Waco: Word Books, 1983.

Hawthorne, G. F., R. P. Martin, and D. G. Reid, eds. *Dictionary of Paul and His Letters.* Downers Grove, Ill.: InterVarsity, 1993.

Hengel, Martin, and Anna Maria Schwemer. *Paul Between Damascus and Antioch: The Unknown Years.* Translated by John Bowden. London: SCM, 1997.

Hermann, Ingo. *Kyrios und Pneuma: Studien zur Christologi der Paulinischen Hauptbriefe.* Studien zur Umwelt des Neuen Testaments 2. Munich: Kösel-Verlag, 1961.

Hurtado, Larry W. *How on Earth Did Jesus Become a God? Historical Questions about Earliest Devotion to Jesus.* Grand Rapids: Eerdmans, 2005.

———. *Lord Jesus Christ: Devotion to Jesus in Earliest Christianity.* Grand Rapids: Eerdmans, 2003.

———. *One God, One Lord: Early Christian Devotion and Ancient Jewish Monotheism.* Philadelphia: Fortress, 1988. 2d ed. Edinburgh: T & T Clark, 1998.

———. "The Binitarian Shape of Early Christian Worship." Pages 187–213 in *The Jewish Roots of Christological Monotheism: Papers from the St. Andrews Conference on the Historical Origins of the Worship of Jesus.* Edited by Carey C. Newman, James R. Davila, and Gladys S. Lewis. Leiden: E. J. Brill, 1999.

———. "First Century Jewish Monotheism." *Journal for the Study of the New Testament* 71 (1998): 3–26. Repr. pages 111–33 in Larry W. Hurtado. *How on Earth Did Jesus Become a God? Historical Questions about Earliest Devotion to Jesus.* Grand Rapids: Eerdmans, 2005.

———. "God." Pages 270–76 in *Dictionary of Jesus and the Gospels.* Edited by J. B. Green, S. McKnight, and I. H. Marshall. Downers Grove, Ill.: InterVarsity, 1992.

———. " 'Jesus' as God's Name, and Jesus as God's Embodied Name in Justin Martyr." Pages 128–36 in *Justin Martyr and His Worlds.* Edited by Sara Parvis and Paul Foster. Minneapolis: Fortress, 2007.

———. "Jesus as Lordly Example in Philippians 2:5-11." Pages 113–26 in *From Jesus to Paul: Studies in Honour of Francis Wright Beare.* Edited by P. Richardson and J. C. Hurd. Waterloo: Wilfrid Laurier University Press, 1984.

———. "Jesus' Divine Sonship in Paul's Epistle to the Romans." Pages 217–33 in *Romans and the People of God.* Edited by Sven K. Soderlund and N. T. Wright. Grand Rapids: Eerdmans, 1999.

———. "Lord." Pages 560–69 in *Dictionary of Paul and His Letters.* Edited by G. F. Hawthorne, R. P. Martin, and D. G. Reid. Downers Grove, Ill.: InterVarsity, 1993.

————. "Pre-Existence." Pages 743–46 in *Dictionary of Paul and His Letters*. Edited by G. F. Hawthorne, R. P. Martin, and D. G. Reid. Downers Grove, Ill.: InterVarsity, 1993.

————. "Pre-70 CE Jewish Opposition to Christ-Devotion." *Journal of Theological Studies* 50, no. 1 (1999): 35–58. Repr. pages 152–78 in *How on Earth Did Jesus Become a God? Historical Questions about Earliest Devotion to Jesus*. Grand Rapids: Eerdmans, 2005.

————. "Remembering and Revelation: The Historic and Glorified Jesus in the Gospel of John." Pages 195–213 in *Israel's God and Rebecca's Children: Essays in Honor of Larry W. Hurtado and Alan F. Segal*. Edited by David B. Capes, April D. DeConick, Helen K. Bond, and Troy A. Miller. Waco: Baylor University Press, 2007.

Jenni, Ernst, and Claus Westermann, eds. *Theological Lexicon of the Old Testament*. Translated by M. E. Biddle. 3 vols. Peabody, Mass.: Hendrickson, 1997.

Jungmann, Joseph. *The Place of Christ in Liturgical Prayer*. 2d and rev. ed. London/Dublin: Geoffrey Chapman, 1965.

Käsemann, Ernst. "A Critical Analysis of Philippians 2:5-11." Pages 45–88 in *God and Christ: Existence and Province*. Edited by R. W. Funk. New York: Harper, 1968.

Kiley, Mark, ed. *Prayer from Alexander to Constantine: A Critical Anthology*. London: Routledge, 1997.

Kingsbury, Jack Dean. " 'God' within the Narrative World of Mark." Pages 75–89 in *The Forgotten God: Perspectives in Biblical Theology*. Edited by A. Andrew Das and Frank J. Matera. Louisville: Westminster John Knox, 2002.

Kirchschläger, W. "ἐπικαλέω." Pages 28–29 in vol. 2 of *Exegetical Dictionary of the New Testament*. Edited by Horst Balz and Gerhard Schneider. Translated by James W. Thompson and John W. Medendorp. 3 vols. Grand Rapids: Eerdmans, 1990–1993.

Kittel, Gerhard, and Gerhard Friedrich, eds. *Theological Dictionary of the New Testament*. Translated by G. W. Bromiley. 10 vols. Grand Rapids: Eerdmans, 1964–1976.

Klumbies, Paul-Gerhard. *Die Rede von Gott bei Paulus in ihrem zeitgeschichtlichen Kontext*. Forschungen zur Religion und Literatur des Alten und Neuen Testaments 155. Göttingen: Vandenhoeck & Ruprecht, 1992.

Kornemann, Ernst. *Doppelprinzipat und Reichsteilung im Imperium Romanum*. Leipzig/Berlin: B. G. Teubner, 1930.

Kreitzer, Larry J. *Jesus and God in Paul's Eschatology*. Journal for the Study of the New Testament: Supplement Series 19. Sheffield: JSOT, 1987.

Kremer, Jacob. "πνεῦμα." Page 118 in vol. 3 of *Exegetical Dictionary of the New Testament*. Edited by Horst Balz and Gerhard Schneider. Translated by James W. Thompson and John W. Medendorp. 3 vols. Grand Rapids: Eerdmans, 1990–1993.

Krentz, Edgar. "God in the New Testament." Pages 75–90 in *Our Naming of God*. Edited by C. E. Braaten. Minneapolis: Fortress, 1989.

Lampe, G. W. H. "The Holy Spirit in the Writings of St. Luke." Pages 159–200 in *Studies in the Gospels: Essays in Memory of R. H. Lightfoot*. Edited by Dennis E. Nineham. Oxford: Basil Blackwell, 1967.

Larsson, Tord. *God in the Fourth Gospel: A Hermeneutical Discussion of the History of Interpretation*. Coniectanea Biblica: NT Series 35. Lund: Almqvist & Wiksell, 2001.

Levison, John R. *Filled with the Spirit*. Grand Rapids: Eerdmans, 2009.

————. *The Spirit in First-Century Judaism*. Arbeiten zur Geschichte des antiken Judentums und des Urchristentums 29. Leiden: E. J. Brill, 1997.

Lindemann, Andreas. "Die Rede von Gott in der paulinische Theologie." *Theologie und Glaube* 69 (1979): 357–76.

Logan, Alistair. *Gnostic Truth and Christian Heresy*. Edinburgh: T & T Clark, 1996.

Lösch, Stephan. *Deitas Jesu und antike Apotheose: Ein Beitrag zur Exegese und Religionsgeschichte*. Rottenburg: Bader'sche Verlagsbuchhandlung, 1933.

Machen, J. Gresham. "The God of the Early Christians." *Princeton Theological Review* 22 (1924): 544–88.

Martin, R. P., and P. H. Davids, eds. *Dictionary of the Later New Testament and Its Developments*. Downers Grove, Ill.: InterVarsity, 1997.

Martyn, J. L. *History and Theology in the Fourth Gospel*. Rev. ed. Nashville: Abingdon Press, 1979.

McGiffert, Arthur Cushman. *The God of the Early Christians*. Edinburgh: T & T Clark, 1924.

Menzies, Robert P. *The Development of Early Christian Pneumatology with Special Reference to Luke-Acts*. Journal for the Study of the New Testament: Supplement Series 54. Sheffield: Sheffield Academic, 1991.

Metzger, Bruce M. *A Textual Commentary on the Greek New Testament*. 2d ed. London/New York: United Bible Societies, 1994.

Meyer, Paul W. " 'The Father': The Presentation of God in the Fourth Gospel." Pages 255–73 in *Exploring the Gospel of John: In Honor of D. Moody Smith*. Edited by R. Alan Culpepper and C. Clifton Black. Louisville: Westminster John Knox, 1996.

Moloney, Francis J. "Telling God's Story: The Fourth Gospel." Pages 107–22 in *The Forgotten God: Perspectives in Biblical Theology*. Edited by A. Andrew Das and Frank J. Matera. Louisville: Westminster John Knox, 2002.

Moore, George Foot. *Judaism in the First Centuries of the Christian Era*. 2 vols. Cambridge, Mass.: Harvard University Press, 1927–30.

Moule, C. F. D. *Worship in the New Testament*. Bramcote: Grove Books, 1983.

Mowery, R. L. "God, Lord and Father: The Theology of the Gospel of Matthew." *Biblical Research* 33 (1988): 24–36.

Moxnes, Halvor. *Theology in Conflict: Studies in Paul's Understanding of God in Romans*. Novum Testamentum Supplements 53. Leiden: E. J. Brill, 1980.

Mussner, Franz. *Der Galaterbrief*. 3d edition. Freiburg: Herder, 1977.

Newman, Carey C. *Paul's Glory-Christology: Tradition and Rhetoric*. Novum Testamentum Supplements 69. Leiden: E. J. Brill, 1992.

———. "God." Pages 412–31 in *Dictionary of the Later New Testament and Its Developments*. Edited by R. P. Martin and P. H. Davids. Downers Grove, Ill.: InterVarsity, 1997.

Neyrey, Jerome H. *Render to God: New Testament Understandings of the Divine*. Minneapolis: Fortress, 2004.

Nickelsburg, G. W. E. *Resurrection, Immortality, and Eternal Life in Intertestamental Judaism and Early Christianity*. Harvard Theological Studies 56. Enlarged edition. Cambridge: Harvard Divinity School, 2006.

North, John A. "Pagans, Polytheists and the Pendulum." Pages 125–45 in *The Spread of Christianity in the First Four Centuries: Essays in Explanation*. Edited by William V. Harris. Leiden: E. J. Brill, 2005.

O'Brien, Peter T. *Introductory Thanksgivings in the Letters of Paul*. Novum Testamentum Supplements 49. Leiden: E. J. Brill, 1977.

Osborn, Eric. *The Emergence of Christian Theology*. Cambridge: Cambridge University Press, 1993.

Pétrement, Simone. *A Separate God: The Christian Origins of Gnosticism.* Translated by Carol Harrison. San Francisco: HarperSanFrancisco, 1990.

Price, S. R. F. "Gods and Emperors: The Greek Language of the Roman Imperial Cult." *Journal of Hellenic Studies* 104 (1984): 79–95.

Reed, David A. *"In Jesus' Name": The History and Beliefs of Oneness Pentecostals. Journal of Pentecostal Theology Supplement Series.* Blandford Forum: Deo Publishing, 2008.

Reese, James M. "The Principal Model of God in the New Testament." *Biblical Theology Bulletin* 8 (1978): 126–31.

Richardson, Neil. *God in the New Testament.* Peterborough: Epworth, 1999.

———. *Paul's Language about God.* Journal for the Study of the New Testament: Supplement Series 99. Sheffield: Sheffield Academic, 1994.

Roberts, Alexander, and James Donaldson, eds. *The Ante-Nicene Fathers.* 1885–1887. 10 vols. Repr. Peabody, Mass.: Hendrickson, 1994.

Rowe, C. Kavin. "New Testament Theology: The Revival of a Discipline: A Review of Recent Contributions to the Field." *Journal of Biblical Literature* 125 (2006): 393–419.

Ruth, Lester. "Lex Amandi, Lex Orandi: The Trinity in the Most-Used Contemporary Christian Worship Songs." Pages 342–59 in *The Place of Christ in Liturgical Prayer: Trinity, Christology, and Liturgical Theology.* Edited by Bryan D. Spinks. Collegeville, Minn.: Liturgical, 2008.

Sand, A. "απαρχη." Pages 116–17 in vol. 1 of *Exegetical Dictionary of the New Testament.* Edited by Horst Balz and Gerhard Schneider. Translated by James W. Thompson and John W. Medendorp. 3 vols. Grand Rapids: Eerdmans, 1990–1993.

———. "αρραβων." Pages 157–58 in vol. 1 of *Exegetical Dictionary of the New Testament.* Edited by Horst Balz and Gerhard Schneider. Translated by James W. Thompson and John W. Medendorp. 3 vols. Grand Rapids: Eerdmans, 1990–1993.

Sanders, E. P. *Paul and Palestinian Judaism.* Philadelphia: Fortress; London: SCM, 1977.

Scholtissek, Klaus. "Er ist nicht ein Gott der Toten, sondern der Lebenden (Mk 12,27). Grundzüge markinischer Theologie." Pages 71–100 in *Der lebendige Gott. Studien zur Theologie des Neuen Testaments: Festschrift für Wilhelm Thüsing zum 75.* Edited by Thomas Söding. Münster: Aschendorf, 1996.

Schüssler Fiorenza, Elisabeth. "Wisdom Mythology and the Christological Hymns of the New Testament." Pages 17–41 in *Aspects of Wisdom in Judaism and Early Christianity.* Edited by R. L. Wilken. Notre Dame: University of Notre Dame Press, 1975.

Scott, Ernest F. *The Spirit in the New Testament.* London: Hodder and Stoughton, 1923.

Segal, Alan F. *Life after Death: A History of the Afterlife in Western Religion.* New York: Doubleday, 2004.

Sekki, Arthur Everett. *The Meaning of Ruah at Qumran.* Society of Biblical Literature Dissertation Series 110. Atlanta: Scholars, 1989.

Sjöberg, Erik. "πνευμα." Page 381 in vol. 6 of *Theological Dictionary of the New Testament.* Edited by Gerhard Kittel and Gerhard Friedrich. Translated by G. W. Bromiley. 10 vols. Grand Rapids: Eerdmans, 1964–1976.

Smith, C. Drew. "The Theology of the Gospel of Mark: A Literary-Theological Investigation Into the Presentation of God in the Second Gospel." PhD diss., University of Edinburgh, 2004.

———. "'This Is My Beloved Son: Listen to Him': Theology and Christology in the Gospel of Mark." *HBT* 24 (2002): 53–86.

Stander, Hendrik F., "Marcion." Pages 715–17 in *Encyclopedia of Early Christianity*. Edited by Everett Ferguson. 2d ed. New York: Garland, 1990.

Stettler, Christian. *Der Kolosserhymnus: Untersuchungen zu Form, traditionsgeschichtlichem Hintergrund und Aussage von Kol 1,15-20*. Wissenschaftliche Untersuchungen zum Neuen Testament. Reihe 2/131. Tübingen: Mohr Siebeck, 2000.

Stuckenbruck, Loren T. *Angel Veneration and Christology: A Study in Early Judaism and in the Christology of the Apocalypse of John*. Wissenschaftliche Untersuchungen zum Neuen Testament. Reihe 2/70. Tübingen: Mohr Siebeck, 1995.

Swete, Henry Barclay. *The Holy Spirit in the New Testament*. London: Macmillan, 1909.

Tepper, Yotam, and Leah Di Segni. *A Christian Prayer Hall of the Third Century CE at Kefar 'Othnay (Legio): Excavations at the Megiddo Prison 2005*. Jerusalem: Israel Antiquities Authority, 2006.

Thiselton, Anthony C. *The First Epistle to the Corinthians*. New International Greek Testament Commentary. Grand Rapids: Eerdmans, 2000.

Thompson, Marianne Meye. *The God of the Gospel of John*. Grand Rapids: Eerdmans, 2001.

———. *The Promise of the Father: Jesus and God in the New Testament*. Louisville: Westminster John Knox, 2000.

Thrall, Margaret E. *The Second Epistle to the Corinthians, Volume 1*. International Critical Commentary. Edinburgh, 1994.

Turner, Max. *Lord of the Spirit: Monotheism, Christology, and Trinitarian Worship in the New Testament*. Milton Keynes: Paternoster, 2007.

———. "The Spirit of Christ and Christology." Pages 168–90 in *Christ the Lord: Studies Presented to Donald Guthrie*. Edited by H. H. Rowdon. Leicester: InterVarsity, 1982.

———. "The Spirit of Christ and 'Divine' Christology." Pages 413–36 in *Jesus of Nazareth, Lord and Christ*. Edited by Joel B. Green and Max Turner. Grand Rapids: Eerdmans, 1994.

VanGemeren, W. A., ed. *New International Dictionary of Old Testament Theology and Exegesis*. 5 vols. Grand Rapids: Eerdmans, 1997.

Van Pelt, Miles V., Walter C. Kaiser, Jr., and Daniel Block. "רוּחַ." Pages 1073–78 in vol. 3 of *New International Dictionary of Old Testament Theology and Exegesis*. Edited by W. A. VanGemeren. 5 vols. Grand Rapids: Eerdmans, 1997.

Varghese, Baby. "Prayers Addressed to Christ in the West Syrian Tradition." Pages 88–111 in *The Place of Christ in Liturgical Prayer: Trinity, Christology, and Liturgical Theology*. Edited by Bryan D. Spinks. Collegeville, Minn.: Liturgical, 2008.

Vouga, François. "Habt Glauben an Gott. Der Theozentrismus der Verkündigung des Evangeliums und des christlichen Glaubens im Markusevangelium." Pages 93–109 in *Texts and Contexts: Biblical Texts in Their Textual and Situational Contexts. Essays in Honor of Lars Hartman*. Edited by Tord Fornberg and David Hellholm. Oslo: Scandinavian Universities Press, 1995.

Wainwright, A. W. *The Trinity in the New Testament*. London: SPCK, 1969.

Watson, Francis. "The Triune Divine Identity: Reflections on Pauline God-Language, in Disagreement with J. D. G. Dunn." *Journal for the Study of the New Testament* 80 (2000): 99–124.

Weima, Jeffrey A. D. *Neglected Endings: The Significance of the Pauline Letter Closings*. Journal for the Study of the New Testament: Supplement Series 101. Sheffield: JSOT, 1994.

Williams, Michael A. *Rethinking "Gnosticism": An Argument for Dismantling a Dubious Category*. Princeton: Princeton University Press, 1996.

Wright, David F. "Trinity." Pages 1142–47 in *Encyclopedia of Early Christianity*. Edited by Everett Ferguson. 2d ed. New York: Garland, 1990.

Wu, J. L. "Liturgical Elements." Pages 557–60 in *Dictionary of Paul and His Letters*. Edited by G. F. Hawthorne, R. P. Martin, and D. G. Reid. Downers Grove, Ill.: InterVarsity, 1993.

Zimmermann, Christiane. *Die Namen des Vaters: Studien zu ausgewälten neutestamentlichen Gottesbezeichnungen vor ihrem frühjüdischen und paganen Sprachhorizont*. Ancient Judaism and Early Christianity 69. Leiden: E. J. Brill, 2007.

INDEX OF SCRIPTURES
AND OTHER ANCIENT
WRITINGS

OLD TESTAMENT

NEW TESTAMENT

6:25-33 36
6:26 . . . . 20, 39, 96
6:32 96
7:11 96
8:16 73
10:1 73
10:1-42 51
10:20 96
10:29-32 . . . . 20, 39
10:32-33 69
11:27-28 . . . . 122n8
12:28 . . . . 57, 82
12:43 73
12:45 73
12:50 . . . . 20, 39
14:22-33 51
26:29 . . . . 20, 39
26:41 73
27:50 73

Mark

1:1-15 . . . . 18, 19
1:1–16:8 18
1:9-11 57
1:11 37
1:11-13 66
1:12 . . . . 80, 130n12
1:14 66
1:14-15 . . . . 51, 59
1:15 37
1:16-20 51
2:1-12 51
3:11 59
3:13-19 51
3:22 51
3:28 . . . . 123n13
3:35 . . . . 20, 39
6:16 . . . . 123n13
8:31-33 51
8:38 . . . . 69, 96
10:45 56
11:25 96
12:13-34 18
12:26-27 31
12:28-30 32
13:13 53
13:32 96

14:25 . . . . 20, 39
14:36 . . . . 37, 56, 96

Luke

3:16 . . . . 79, 82, 89
4:1 . . . . 80, 130n12
6:35 . . . . 20, 39
6:36 96
9:26 96
10:21-22 96
10:22 . . . . 122n8
11:2 . . . . 40, 96
11:20 . . . . 57, 82
12:6-8 . . . . 20, 39
12:8-9 69
12:24 . . . . 20, 39

John

1:1 54
1:1-3 . . . . 43, 65, 122n8
1:1-18 . . . . 3, 66
1:12-13 40
1:14 . . . . 122n8
1:14-18 31
1:17 67
1:18 36
1:36 . . . . 122n8
3:16 36
3:18 . . . . 122n8
3:35 . . . . 39, 96
4:21-23 39
5:17 96
5:18 . . . . 39, 96, 109
5:19-24 40
5:19-45 39
5:20-23 96
5:22-23 109
5:23 . . . . 44, 64
5:26 96
5:30 59
5:36 59
5:36-37 96
5:43 96
6:27-65 39
6:32 39
6:40 39
7:37-39 87

OLD TESTAMENT APOCRYPHA

OLD TESTAMENT PSEUDEPIGRAPHA

DEAD SEA SCROLLS

RABBINIC TEXTS

APOSTOLIC FATHERS

PHILO

TERTULLIAN

THEOPHILUS